Forensics

Other books in The Lucent Library of Science and Technology include:

Artificial Intelligence
Bacteria and Viruses
Black Holes
Cloning
Comets and Asteroids
Computer Viruses
Energy Alternatives
Exploring Mars
Genetics
Global Warming
The Internet
Lasers
Plate Tectonics
Space Stations
Telescopes
Virtual Reality

THE LUCENT LIBRARY OF SCIENCE AND TECHNOLOGY

Forensics

by Gail B. Stewart

I. C. C. LIBRARY

LUCENT BOOKS

An imprint of Thomson Gale, a part of The Thomson Corporation

THOMSON
™
GALE

Detroit • New York • San Francisco • San Diego • New Haven, Conn. • Waterville, Maine • London • Munich

THOMSON

★ ™

GALE

On cover: During a training session, crime scene investigators carefully remove leaves from the body of a dummy representing a murder victim.

LIBRARY OF CONGRESS CATALOGING-IN-PUBLICATION DATA

Stewart, Gail B., 1949–
    Forensics / by Gail B. Stewart
        p. cm. — (The Lucent library of science and technology)
Includes bibliographical references and index.
Contents: Forensics and fingerprints—Who are you?—Crime solving through chemistry—Questioned documents—Crime scene impressions—The DNA fingerprint.
ISBN 1-59018-641-9
1. Forensic sciences—Juvenile literature. 2. Criminal investigation—Juvenile literature. 3. Evidence, criminal—Juvenile literature. I. Title. II. Series.
HV8073.8.S74 2005
363.25—dc22

2005014646

Printed in the United States of America

Table of Contents

Foreword

"The world has changed far more in the past 100 years than in any other century in history. The reason is not political or economic, but technological—technologies that flowed directly from advances in basic science."

— Stephen Hawking, "A Brief History of Relativity," *Time*, 2000

The twentieth-century scientific and technological revolution that British physicist Stephen Hawking describes in the above quote has transformed virtually every aspect of human life at an unprecedented pace. Inventions unimaginable a century ago have not only become commonplace but are now considered necessities of daily life. As science historian James Burke writes, "We live surrounded by objects and systems that we take for granted, but which profoundly affect the way we behave, think, work, play, and in general conduct our lives."

For example, in just one hundred years, transportation systems have dramatically changed. In 1900 the first gasoline-powered motorcar had just been introduced, and only 144 miles of U.S. roads were hard-surfaced. Horse-drawn trolleys still filled the streets of American cities. The airplane had yet to be invented. Today 217 million vehicles speed along 4 million miles of U.S. roads. Humans have flown to the moon and commercial aircraft are capable of transporting passengers across the Atlantic Ocean in less than three hours.

The transformation of communications has been just as dramatic. In 1900 most Americans lived and worked on farms without electricity or mail delivery. Few people had ever heard a radio or spoken on a telephone. A hundred years later, 98 percent of American homes have telephones and televisions and more than 50 percent have personal computers. Some families even have more than one television and computer, and cell phones are now commonplace, even among the young. Data beamed from communication satellites routinely predict global weather conditions, and fiber-optic cable, e-mail, and the Internet have made worldwide telecommunication instantaneous.

Perhaps the most striking measure of scientific and technological change can be seen in medicine and public health. At the beginning of the twentieth century, the average American life span was forty-seven years. By the end of the century the average life span was approaching eighty years, thanks to advances in medicine including the development of vaccines and antibiotics, the discovery of powerful diagnostic tools such as X rays, the lifesaving technology of cardiac and neonatal care, improvements in nutrition, and the control of infectious disease.

Rapid change is likely to continue throughout the twenty-first century as science reveals more about physical and biological processes such as global warming, viral replication, and electrical conductivity, and as people apply that new knowledge to personal decisions and government policy. Already, for example, an international treaty calls for immediate reductions in industrial and automobile emissions in response to studies that show a potentially dangerous rise in global temperatures is caused by human activity. Taking an active role in determining the direction of future changes depends on education; people must understand the possible uses of scientific research and the effects of the technology that surrounds them.

The Lucent Books Library of Science and Technology profiles key innovations and discoveries that have transformed the modern world. Each title strives to make a complex scientific discovery, technology, or phenomenon understandable and relevant to the reader. Because scientific discovery is rarely straightforward, each title explains the dead ends, fortunate accidents, and basic scientific methods by which the research into the subject proceeded. And every book examines the practical applications of an invention, branch of science, or scientific principle in industry, public health, and personal life, as well as potential future uses and effects based on ongoing research. Fully documented quotations, annotated bibliographies that include both print and electronic sources, glossaries, indexes, and technical illustrations are among the supplemental features designed to point researchers to further exploration of the subject.

Where Science Meets Crime

Only a century ago, it was rare that evidence alone proved that a criminal was guilty. Many crimes were solved by eyewitnesses or by the criminal's confession. "You do hear about cases [in the late nineteenth century] where a murderer left a bloody fingerprint, or maybe the police chased down a fleeing suspect who had a bloodstained knife or something, and just like that, they had their evidence," says Dave, a retired police officer. "But otherwise, those guys didn't get caught very often in real life."

It was not that criminals did not leave evidence, he insists. "No, it was there, same as today, same as every crime scene," he says. "But law enforcement didn't have science on their side back then. They didn't know about DNA, or how to lift latent fingerprints with super glue, or how to establish the time of death of a murder victim, or any of the things investigators take for granted today. Forensics makes it a whole different story."[1]

"All They Need Is the Smoke"

Forensics, a term that is short for "forensic science," is the application of science and technology to matters of interest to the legal system, especially criminal cases. While most of these scientific instruments

Scientists at the FBI forensics lab in Quantico, Virginia, study DNA evidence collected from a crime scene.

were designed for other purposes, they have had exciting results in criminal investigation. For example, the powerful new microscopes used in medical research are also used today to examine and identify the fibers found on the bodies of murder victims. Lasers developed to help scientists study molecular structure are now used to illuminate fingerprints that are otherwise invisible. And the study of genetics has revolutionized the criminal justice system with the use of DNA analysis.

New techniques in forensics have created valuable new tools for investigators, tools that can establish a suspect's guilt or prove someone's innocence. No longer must investigators rely solely on evidence that can be seen with the naked eye. As forensic researcher David Fisher notes, "Not long ago, investigators had to find the smoking gun to convict a suspect. Now all they need is the smoke."[2]

Chapter 1

Forensics and Fingerprints

Fingerprint analysis is one of the most widely used forensic tools. No two people on earth have the same fingerprints, and by collecting fingerprints left at a crime scene, police can assemble a virtual "who's who" of individuals who were in that place. A woman who insists that she had never set foot in the hotel room where a murder was committed, for example, can be instantly proved wrong if her fingerprints are found there. Similarly, a man's fingerprint on the trigger of a murder weapon may not prove that he committed the murder, but it is irrefutable evidence that he at least handled the gun.

Since Prehistoric Times

The idea that people's fingerprints differ and therefore can be used as a means of identification is not a new one. In fact, certain ancient cultures believed that a person's fingerprint was the best way to solve disputes over identity. Archaeologists have found fingerprint impressions that acted as a sort of signature on clay tablets used by ancient Babylonians for business transactions. And it was not uncommon for legal documents in ancient China to be sealed with clay—with a clear thumbprint affixed to the seal as a way of personalizing the document.

The use of fingerprints in criminal investigations, however, began far more recently. Only when researchers made two critical discoveries did using fingerprints as a forensic tool become possible. First, they confirmed that no two individuals have the same fingerprints; each person's fingerprints are unique. In fact, even identical twins do not share the same fingerprint patterns.

The second crucial discovery was that fingerprints do not change throughout a person's life. A British

A criminal records specialist combs through fingerprint records in hopes of finding a match to prints found at a crime scene.

Fingerprint Patterns

Fingerprints are a foolproof method of identification because each person's fingerprints are unique, and fingerprints do not change throughout a person's lifetime. Fingerprint ridges appear in three pattern types: loops, whorls, and arches.

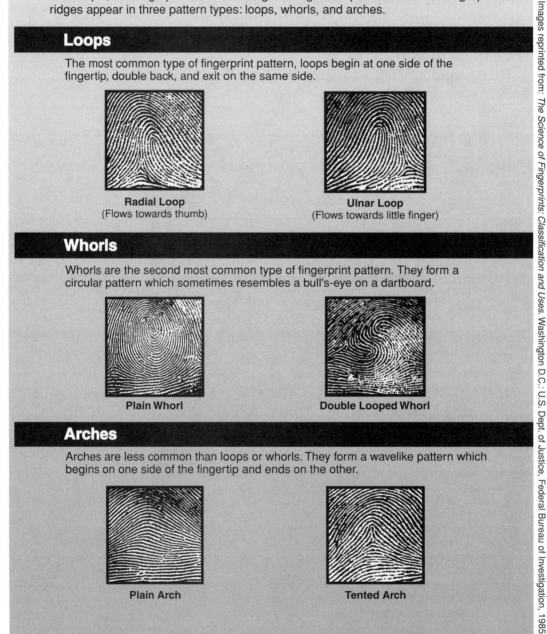

Loops

The most common type of fingerprint pattern, loops begin at one side of the fingertip, double back, and exit on the same side.

Radial Loop
(Flows towards thumb)

Ulnar Loop
(Flows towards little finger)

Whorls

Whorls are the second most common type of fingerprint pattern. They form a circular pattern which sometimes resembles a bull's-eye on a dartboard.

Plain Whorl

Double Looped Whorl

Arches

Arches are less common than loops or whorls. They form a wavelike pattern which begins on one side of the fingertip and ends on the other.

Plain Arch

Tented Arch

Images reprinted from: *The Science of Fingerprints: Classification and Uses.* Washington D.C.: U.S. Dept. of Justice, Federal Bureau of Investigation, 1985.

officer serving in India, William Herschel, determined this in 1858 after he began studying certain contracts. He required anyone signing a contract to leave an inked palm print. Herschel noticed that a person's palm print would not change at all from year to year. "From the day you are born until the day you die," adds a forensic researcher, "the only physical aspect of your body that won't change is the shape of those funny lines in your skin."[3] Even when the skin of the fingers is severely burned or damaged, the new skin that eventually replaces the damaged tissue will have the same pattern as before.

Necessary Ridges

By the early twentieth century, prisons in the United States and a few other nations had begun taking inked fingerprint impressions from every inmate as a foolproof way of identifying them. In addition, law enforcement agencies were learning to gather fingerprints from the scene of a crime and store them so that when they had a suspect, they could compare the prints with his or hers. This was the beginning of the use of fingerprints as a forensic tool. Throughout the years, the science of collecting and classifying fingerprints has improved, becoming much more sophisticated.

Yet even with the forensic fingerprint improvements, the basics of the science remain the same. It all boils down to those little lines on the skin of the fingers and the unique patterns they make. The lines, which are raised from the rest of the skin, are called friction ridges, because they give the fingers the ability to grip something smooth. Without such friction ridges, notes forensic specialist D.P. Lyle, "we'd all be butterfingers."[4]

Loops, Whorls, and Arches

Fingerprint experts recognize three main patterns made by the ridges on fingertips. Loops are the most common pattern. In fact, about 60 percent of the patterns on human fingerprints are made up of loops. A loop is a ridge, or series of ridges, that begins at one side of the fingertip, doubles back, and exits on the same side. The next most common pattern is a whorl, which resembles a bull's-eye on a dartboard. Approximately 35 percent of the patterns on fingertips are whorls. The least common, at 5 percent, is an arch. Arches are made up of ridge lines that rise in the middle and form a sort of wave pattern. The lines of an arch differ from a loop in that they begin on one side of the finger and end on the other.

These three ridge patterns can be broken down into subgroups, too. For instance, tented arches are sharper than other arches, forming a point at the top. Examiners can also distinguish between an ulnar loop, which flows toward the little finger, and a radial loop, which flows toward the thumb side. A fingerprint examiner can also see the difference between a whorl that is shaped like a spiral and one formed by two loops that appear to collide and swirl around in a circle.

Individual Ridges

The patterns of ridges are not the only aspect of fingerprints that an examiner looks at. The ridges themselves have various characteristics that can be classified and noted. A bifurcation, for example, occurs when a ridge splits into two separate ridges. "It's like looking at a map where a highway kind of forks off, one way going northeast and another veering off to the northwest," says fingerprint technician Richard. "[Bifurcations] are probably the easiest ridge detail to spot."[5]

Fingerprint examiners also note the presence of islands, or short ridges that start and stop abruptly, and lakes, an opening created when a ridge splits, quickly reconnects, and continues on as a single ridge. "Another easy one to spot we call a railway tie," says Richard. "It's a short ridge that runs perpendicular to two parallel ridges, like a bridge."[6]

Ridge details such as these, combined with the patterns of ridges, are what make each fingerprint unique. "This is why fingerprints are so important," says a police officer who has worked on rape and murder cases. "If you can get a clear print, or at least a partial print, at a crime scene, you have a shot of establishing that that person was, without a doubt, present at that scene. It doesn't mean the person's guilty, but it's an important lead for investigators to follow."[7]

"God Bless Chocoholics"

The trick, however, is to be successful at finding prints at a crime scene. Some prints are easier to spot than others. Patent prints, for example, are made when a person's fingers come into contact with a substance that can leave a visible trace. Substances such as ink, blood, and dirt are easy to pick up on one's fingertips. When a person who has touched such a substance then touches something else, his or her fingerprints become noticeable.

One of the first arrests made because of a fingerprint was in the 1860s in Japan, when a thief left bloody fingerprints on a wall. A man was captured, and because his fingerprints matched those on the wall, he was arrested for the crime. More recently, a Chicago burglar had been eating fast food before he committed his crime and did not realize that he left his ketchup-smeared fingerprints on the windowsill—a mistake that ultimately led to his arrest and conviction.

Impressed prints, sometimes referred to as plastic prints, are also easy to see. These are created when a person's finger presses into a soft substance and leaves a clear impression behind. Police have arrested people whose prints have been found in soft putty, caulking around a window, wax, chewing gum, and even on a bar of soap. One Canadian investigator says that she found the most memorable impressed print one Christmas Day on a piece of chocolate candy that an intruder had taken a bite of and put back in the box:

> This had been a nightmare crime scene—no nonresident prints anywhere. Then, there it was—this beautiful complete thumb print on a piece of chocolate in a Christmas candy box! It's funny how we think sometimes. The suspect touched nothing else, but was caught because he didn't like nuts. God bless chocoholics![8]

Latent Prints

Although patent prints are relatively easy to see, the most common prints left at a crime scene are not visible—at least not to the naked eye. Because they are hidden, they are referred to as latent prints. Latent prints are not created by impressions or by dirt or blood residue on the fingers. Instead, they are caused by the transfer of sweat and other secretions from the skin's pores to the ridges of the fingertips and then to any object a person touches.

Because the prints are not visible, it is difficult for criminals to know what they have touched, and often an inadvertent print will be enough to convict even the most careful perpetrator. FBI fingerprint specialist Danny Greathouse says that experience has taught him to look for prints in places that a criminal is likely to miss.

"In motel rooms, we often find prints on the wall next to the front window, because someone has leaned on it while moving the curtain to look outside," Greathouse explains. He also looks for prints under the toilet seat, where a man would lift it before urinating, and on cigarette butts. In cars, he looks on radio buttons and the lever that adjusts the position of the driver's seat. When examining a gun, he looks at the inside as well as the outside, for people forget that while cleaning the gun they leave prints, too.

No matter how meticulous a criminal is in cleaning up, it is almost impossible to catch every print, Greathouse says. He recalls a bank robbery case in which a gang had been careful to wipe down every

A Forty-Year-Old Fingerprint

Fingerprints are pretty durable evidence, and there is no better proof of this than the case of Valerian Trifa, a former archbishop of the Romanian Orthodox Church. Trifa became a citizen of the United States in 1957. Soon afterward, however, the U.S. Department of Naturalization began getting letters about Trifa that accused him of having been a leader of the Romanian Nazi Party during World War II. In fact, the letters explained, Trifa had been one of the leaders of a horrific killing spree in Bucharest that had ended in the murder of almost six thousand people, most of them Jews. Trifa vehemently denied his affiliation with the Nazis, but his fingerprints proved him a liar. In 1982 the government of West Germany produced a postcard that Trifa had sent to a high-ranking Nazi official in Germany during the war. In that postcard, Trifa pledged his undying loyalty and support to the Nazis. Using a laser light, the FBI forensic lab developed a thumbprint, which matched the print Trifa had given when he had applied for U.S. citizenship. Trifa was deported from the United States in 1984.

The FBI identified Romanian archbishop Valerian Trifa as a Nazi using a forty-year-old fingerprint on a postcard.

square inch of the apartment they had been living in during the planning of the crime. "But when they left," he says, "someone forgot to turn on the dishwasher and we got all their prints off dirty dishes and glasses and silverware."[9]

"Every Scene Is Different"

Of course, it would be extremely time-consuming to process every surface at a crime scene for latent prints. Forensic technicians have found that by shining certain lights on surfaces, latent prints can be seen. One such light is a laser, or very high-energy light source. By turning a laser on a surface, crime scene processors can determine whether a surface is likely to yield latent prints.

For a latent fingerprint to be of value as a forensic tool, however, simply finding it is not enough. It must be developed so that it is visible, and it must be transferred from the surface where it is found to a fingerprint card that can be used later in comparison with a suspect's fingerprints.

Sometimes surfaces believed to contain latent prints are processed at the crime scene, especially large surfaces such as doors, windows, and countertops. Other times, the surfaces require techniques that are best done in a forensic laboratory. In such cases, evidence is carefully packaged to ensure that no scratches or smudges occur en route to the lab that could make a print unreadable.

"Every scene is different," says one Canadian investigator. "One of my instructors tells of removing an entire wall because it was covered in old-fashioned, uncoated wallpaper and he wanted to fume it [use laboratory equipment to bring out the prints]. He turned up the only decent prints of the case."[10]

Powder, Brushes, and Tape

If the surface being fingerprinted is smooth and solid—such as a countertop, a glossy wooden table,

or a metal file cabinet—the most common technique for developing prints is dusting. A technician uses a very soft brush to apply a special powder over the surface. The powder is made of finely ground aluminum, carbon, charcoal, or titanium. The powders vary in color, and a fingerprint specialist chooses one that will contrast with the color of the surface the print is on.

After the powder is carefully brushed onto the surface, it adheres to the tiny bits of sweat, amino acids, and oils secreted through the pores of the skin and left by the ridges of the fingers. Once the technician gently blows away the excess powder, what remains is a fingerprint, the detailed pattern of ridges.

Once the print is dusted and therefore visible, a forensic photographer takes a picture of it. After that, the print is removed, or lifted, from the surface. A technician covers the print with a piece of clear,

A forensic investigator shines a flashlight on the door of a robbed jewelry store to check for fingerprint evidence.

Finding Latent Fingerprints

Latent fingerprints are not visible to the naked eye. Depending on the object and quality of the prints, forensic technicians use different methods to locate and preserve latent prints.

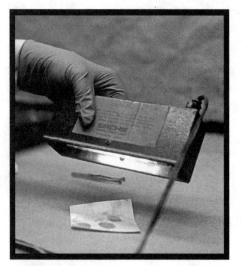

Exposing the fingerprints to a special light will sometimes cause the prints to appear.

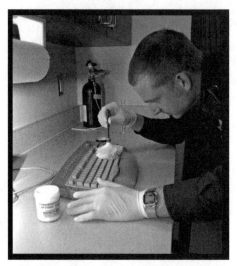

A soft brush is used to dust a fine, colored powder over the surface of the evidence. The powder sticks to the latent prints.

The dusted print is covered with clear, sticky tape and carefully lifted off. The tape is placed on a plastic card for later comparison.

Instead of dusting, various chemicals are sometimes applied to porous materials like paper and cardboard to bring prints into view.

sticky tape and carefully peels the tape off. The print pattern sticks to the tape and is placed on a clear plastic card to be used later in examining and comparing the print with the prints of any individuals who become suspects in the crime.

A New Use for Superglue

In some cases, chemicals are used to develop prints. One of the most widely used is cyanoacrylate, more commonly known as superglue. Quite by accident, a scientist found that when it is heated, superglue releases fumes that stick to amino acids, including the tiny amounts left as fingerprints.

Fingerprint technicians place the evidence in an airtight chamber. "In our lab we have several different ones," says latent print specialist David Peterson of Minnesota's Bureau of Criminal Apprehension (BCA). "It just depends on the size of the evidence. We use one that's about the size of a microwave oven, or if we're working with a shotgun or rifle or something, we've got a long, narrow chamber for that. We even have a big chamber downstairs for fuming large objects—bikes, chairs, things like that."[11]

Inside the chamber, the glue is heated to its boiling point. In just seconds, the glue hardens along the ridges of the print, turning them white. Colored dyes are added to make the print contrast with the background. The prints are then photographed.

Developing Prints on Paper

Superglue works well to take prints from hard surfaces, but when evidence is porous, such as cardboard or paper, technicians are more likely to use a variety of other chemicals to develop latent prints. "The thing is, the oils, the amino acids, the stuff that makes up a fingerprint, it soaks into the paper, rather than stay on the surface, so dusting or even superglue isn't very efficient," says Peterson. "We get prints that are far more clear if we use chemicals, and we've got lots of choices—in all, forty-five different chemicals for different situations. Often you try one, if it doesn't work well, you try something else that's more sensitive."[12]

Some of the chemicals react with the amino acids in the print, others with the oils. Some chemicals, such as ninhydrin and silver nitrate, are especially valuable in retrieving prints from wet or damaged paper. Peterson recalls a recent case in which a fingerprint taken from a soggy piece of paper made all the difference.

"This guy broke into a house, and as he's driving away, he starts throwing stuff out the window of his car," he says. "There was a check register that had one check left in it, and he pitched that right out the window, where it landed in a ditch. Well, it was wet when we recovered it, and we let it dry out and then soaked it in the silver nitrate. It turns the paper black, much like developing a photograph. And when we put a bright light on it, we could see that we had prints.

"Years ago," Peterson says, "no one would have thought that this kind of thing was possible—getting prints off something that's been lying in a ditch covered with water. And now, getting prints off something like that isn't all that unusual."[13]

"Fingerprints Aren't Bar Codes"

Yet even the clearest fingerprint is worthless unless an investigator can compare it with the prints of a suspect. "Remember, fingerprints aren't bar codes," says one police officer. "It's not like we know who the print belongs to by looking at it."[14]

When prints are recovered from a crime scene, they are compared to those of anyone that police may suspect of having committed the crime. If there are no suspects, investigators must broaden their search to fingerprints that are already on file. Checking even those fingerprints in a local police file

Fingerprinting the Dead

In his book *Hard Evidence*, author David Fisher discusses the methods fingerprinting technicians use to help identify dead bodies, especially those that are physically decayed:

> Very often the hands of people who die in accidents are found clenched into tight fists, and while that might be beneficial to specialists because the fingerprints are somewhat protected, first the hands have to be pried open. This can be done forcefully, it can be done by making small cuts in the base of the fingers, or it can be done by severing the hand from the body and heating it in a microwave oven for several minutes.
>
> To return shriveled or badly wrinkled skin to a natural, rounded shape so as to obtain a print, investigators can soak it in water, heat it for a short time in a microwave, or inject it with a chemical substance called tissue builder. Conversely, if a finger is swollen, as it might be if the corpse was a "floater"—a body that has been in the water for a long time—sidelighting will create shadows in the fingerprint valleys, which can then be photographed. If the top layer of skin, the epidermis, has been destroyed or damaged or charred in a fire, it can be cut off, and usable prints can be obtained from the second layer of skin, the dermis.

A forensic technician in Thailand takes the fingerprints of an unidentified victim of the 2004 tsunami.

would be a time-consuming task that could require dozens of examiners with magnifying glasses searching through thousands of cards. And if the search were nationwide, the FBI's more than 65 million fingerprint files would make such painstaking comparison virtually impossible.

Fingerprint comparison was made easier in the 1980s when fingerprint examiners gained a remarkable tool known as the Automated Fingerprint Identification System, or AFIS. An examiner can enter a fingerprint in the system and AFIS will scan it and check the patterns of the ridges against millions of other prints in minutes. Any prints that are possible matches are transmitted to the examiner, who can then compare the ridge detail by hand. "That's an important part," says one forensic technician. "It's not the computer that has the final say—it's a real human, sitting at a desk, looking carefully at two prints side by side. Not until he or she has examined it carefully and is convinced that the two are identical is the fingerprint declared a match."[15]

"You Haven't Printed Everybody in the World"

The match of a suspect's print to a print found at a crime scene is frequently the evidence that can convict a criminal. Fingerprint experts are aware of the importance of this forensic tool. After all, a fingerprint is the only known physical means of establishing a person's identity. Not even DNA is that accurate, since identical twins share it.

"Sometimes I get asked, 'How do you *know* there aren't two people with the same fingerprints? You haven't printed everybody in the world,'" says David Peterson of the BCA. "Well, right, we haven't printed everyone. And we're not going to. But I can show you a database right here in Minnesota that has 10 million fingerprints on it, and no two match. That's pretty awesome. In one hundred years that the science [of fingerprint examination] has existed, we've

never found two persons who have the same fingerprints."[16]

FBI fingerprint expert Danny Greathouse agrees,
and explains that fingerprints have become the most
solid type of evidence in criminal court cases, so
much so that without the irrefutable reputation of a
fingerprint, criminal justice would be decimated.
"The day we find two prints that we can't tell apart,"
he says, "that'll be the day we close the door and
walk out of here forever, because we'll be out of business."[17]

Chapter 2

Who Are You?

Whereas fingerprints are often used to find the identity of a criminal, bones and teeth are often examined by forensic scientists to determine the identity of a victim. "Sometimes, a photograph doesn't help you identify someone," says one police officer, "in the case of a fire or a plane crash or something like that: Sometimes it may be a body that's discovered—maybe it's been there so long it's just skeletal remains. In those cases visual identification is impossible, so teeth and bones are the only thing investigators can go on."[18]

"Teeth Are Terrific"

The idea of using teeth to identify human remains is not new. In fact, one of the first cases on record occurred during the Revolutionary War. In the bloody Battle of Bunker Hill, 140 colonists died and were buried in a mass grave. Later, however, the family of one of the men, Dr. Joseph Warren, asked that his body be disinterred so that he could be buried in the family plot.

By that time, it was extremely difficult to distinguish the remains of any one man from those of the others in the grave. However, just a few months before the battle, Warren had had some dentures made. The man who made them was Paul Revere, who in addition to being a silversmith was also a part-time dentist. He was able to make a positive identification of Warren.

Warren was remarkable in that he had dental work; the vast majority of eighteenth-century Americans did not visit dentists. But most people today do, and as a result, they have dental records on file. When an unknown body is brought in to be autopsied and identified, investigators know they will have far more luck getting a positive identification from dental work than any other means. "Teeth are terrific," says one forensic specialist. "Give us one tooth and we just might be able to make an identification. Give us a mouthful and we can often match suspects to victims, unknowns to names."[19]

A Lot of Information

A surprising amount of information can be learned from examining the teeth. Forensic dentists usually take a full set of dental X-rays of an unknown victim, and from the number and position of certain

An investigator studies dental X-rays to make a positive identification of a tsunami victim in Thailand.

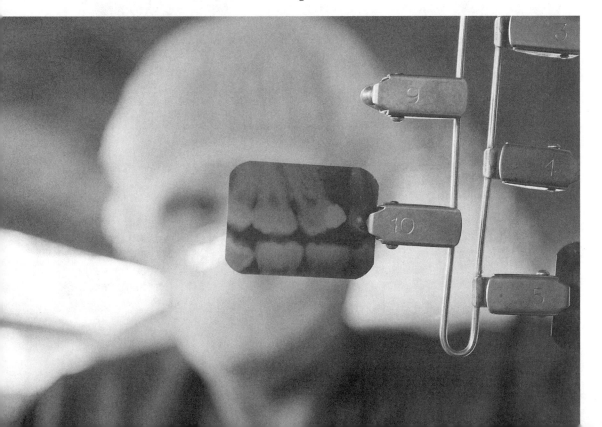

Dental Identification

Forensic experts use dental remains to name victims who cannot otherwise be identified. When comparing remains to official dental records, experts will compare the locations of any chipped, missing, or filled teeth, along with bite patterns and other identifying characterisitics.

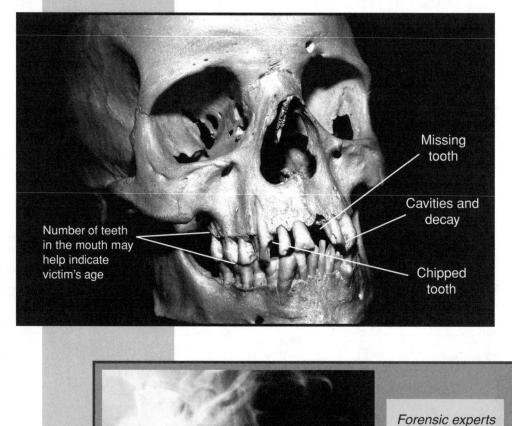

Missing tooth

Cavities and decay

Chipped tooth

Number of teeth in the mouth may help indicate victim's age

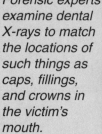

Forensic experts examine dental X-rays to match the locations of such things as caps, fillings, and crowns in the victim's mouth.

teeth, they can often determine an approximate age. For instance, if the roots of the teeth are shallow, dentists know that the permanent teeth have not yet come in, and thus the remains belong to a child. Because there is an order in which the permanent teeth come in, dentists can be fairly accurate at guessing the age of the child.

Adult teeth on an X-ray can provide clues as well, such as excessive wear on tooth surfaces, evidence of gum disease, or pulled teeth. Teeth can also hint at certain health problems. One young woman who was believed to have perished in a house fire in New York in the late 1990s had suffered from bulimia, an eating disorder in which she forced herself to vomit after eating. Little but bones and teeth remained after the fire, but forensic dentists found two clues that pointed them toward the missing girl. First, although most of the teeth were permanent, the wisdom teeth had not yet come in, something that usually occurs in the late teens or early twenties. Second, and more compelling, the teeth had little enamel, which made it a strong possibility that the person had been bulimic since the stomach acid from so much vomiting strips the enamel from teeth.

No Dental Database

After a forensic dentist examines the teeth, a full set of X-rays is taken. In cases in which investigators believe they know who the person is, the task of verification is usually fairly simple. "We ask the police if they have an idea of who this was," says Ramsey County, Minnesota, medical examiner Dr. Michael McGee. "Then we go to the dentist and ask for the X-rays of Mary Johnson, or whoever.

"Dentists keep track of the condition of the teeth—whether it's chipped or missing teeth, fillings, root canals, crowns, and so on. And many people get a set of X-rays taken once every year or so. If that's the case, then a comparison is done. Of course, it's much more difficult if there are no likely ideas of who the person was. There is no dental database like there is for fingerprints."[20]

Tooth Number 18

Sometimes even when investigators have a good idea of the identity of the body, the comparison can be difficult. "If you don't have a full set of teeth, that can make it hard for the forensic people," says one police officer. "There have been cases where the victim had only a few teeth, and unless there is something really remarkable about them, it's pretty hard for any forensic examiner to say with certainty that they have an ID."[21]

In one case in Minnesota, however, an identification was made on the basis of a single tooth—and a great deal of luck. Nineteen-year-old Katie Poirier was abducted from the convenience store where she worked in rural Moose Lake, and it was believed she had been murdered. When human remains were found in a fire pit on land belonging to a suspect, investigators thought they might be those of Poirier. Hoping that teeth had survived the fire, they were eager to make a positive identification.

The fire pit contained very little, however—only a few charred bones and a single tooth. At first glance, forensic dentists were less than optimistic. The tooth was what is called "tooth number 18," which means that on a dental chart, it would be the molar in the lower left part of the mouth. The tooth had a filling in it, which might have been helpful if the forensic dentists had a view of the person's complete set of teeth; the chances of a single filled tooth yielding much information were almost nil.

"Imagine the Odds"

When investigators looked at Poirier's dental records, they saw that that molar had been filled. In fact, the dental work had been done just ten days before her abduction. Her dentist said that he had replaced an old filling that day and had used a sample of a brand-new dental adhesive he had been given at a recent dentists' convention. The new product contained a substance called zirconium, and, at the time, it was the only product on the market with that ingredient.

When the forensic dentists examined the tooth from the fire pit under a powerful scanning microscope, they found traces of zirconium on it. Because of the rarity of that substance, and because it was found on tooth number 18, investigators were confident in stating that the remains were those of Katie Poirier. Says one police officer, "It's incredibly hard to imagine the odds of finding that particular tooth which was so unique. That really provided the positive ID the police and Katie's family were looking for."[22]

The Bone Detectives

Though bones are not quite as long lasting as teeth, they can yield far more information for investigators trying to make an identification. Forensic examiners who deal with skeletal remains are called forensic anthropologists, or, sometimes, "bone detectives." They pride themselves on their ability to find clues in bones long after the flesh and organs have decomposed. As noted forensic anthropologist Dr. Douglas Ubelaker explains:

Experienced forensic anthropologists have examined thousands of bones from all time periods and from all over the world. . . . They know what happens to a skeleton after the passage of a month, a decade, a century, two thousand years. They know what happens when a skeleton is left on the prairie after an Indian massacre, and buried years later by a passer-by. They can distinguish between evidence of murder and the results of a dog passing by and helping himself to lunch.[23]

More than five thousand sets of skeletal remains are found each year in the United States. Some are hundreds of years old, such as the remains found when an old burial ground is accidentally dug up. Others are more recent, such as bones of people who died in a fiery airplane crash or those of a victim of a crime whose body was purposely hidden. "Especially if a crime has been committed, if the remains belong to a victim who's never been identified, it's critical to learn all we can," says one young woman who is studying to be a forensic scientist. "It's amazing how much the bone [detectives] can tell you about who that person was. You read about some of the cases these people have worked on, and it's like the bones speak to [the forensic anthropologists] in a language that only they can understand. It's uncanny."[24]

Human?

The first task when remains are found is determining whether they are human or not. The distinction between animal bones and human ones is not as easy as one might think, say experts. For example, the bones of a bear's front paws look very much like those of human hands, and the fragments of a turtle shell are often mistaken for pieces of a human skull.

One bone detective says that as a medical student he was once called to a home where some people had found a mysterious skull in a compost heap in their backyard. Although he was just about to sit down to Thanksgiving dinner, he went to investigate, and found the experience so fascinating that he decided to pursue a career as a forensic anthropologist:

I missed Thanksgiving dinner and spent half the afternoon excavating a pile of rotten kitchen refuse, all to uncover a cat's skeleton. They were afraid it was an infant. Didn't take more than a glance to assure them that it wasn't but somehow, in the time it took to get that skull out of the garbage, I was hooked.[25]

Determining Sex

Once the remains are found to be human, bone detectives can determine the sex of such remains.

Identifying Josef Mengele

Forensic anthropology was employed in 1985 to determine whether remains found in Brazil belonged to former Nazi war criminal Dr. Josef Mengele. Mengele had been known as "the Angel of Death" because of his cruel experiments on inmates of Nazi death camps. He had personally overseen the deaths of at least 400,000 people.

Forensic specialists from the United States, Austria, and Germany examined the skeleton. From the skull's eye holes and jaw, they decided the skull belonged to a white male. The length of the skeleton seemed right for Mengele's size, and the bones indicated that the person was nearly seventy at the time of death, which matched Mengele's age.

The most compelling evidence was the superimposing of a photograph of Mengele onto a photograph of the skull of the skeleton. There were thirty points at which the bones matched, enough for the three forensic examiners to declare the remains to be Mengele. Later, a 1992 DNA analysis of the bones matched DNA from Mengele's living relatives in Germany, proving that the forensic anthropologists had been correct in their findings.

In 1992 a forensics team identified skeletal remains found in Brazil as those of Nazi doctor Josef Mengele.

Though men and women have the same 206 bones in their bodies, there are definite differences in the look of those bones. One obvious difference is that the bones of a male are thicker and more dense than female bones. "[A man's] bones are thick, pitted, and bumped with rough irregularities where the muscles and tendons were attached," says forensic anthropologist William Maples. On the other hand, the bones of a female tend to be smoother, he says, "with edges gracefully planed or beveled."[26]

Those differences, however, can blur in certain situations. A transsexual man who takes estrogen, for instance, will develop a smoother skeleton over time. Conversely, some female bodybuilders create the same knotty lumps that males have on the bones of their arms and legs as they develop more muscle.

If the pelvic bones are intact, experts say that they can easily tell if they are female bones. A female pelvis is wider, since the bones need to be able to allow the passage of a baby during birth. The back side

Forensic scientists examine the bones of children found in a mass grave in England in 2005. Their skeletal remains will help determine their ages.

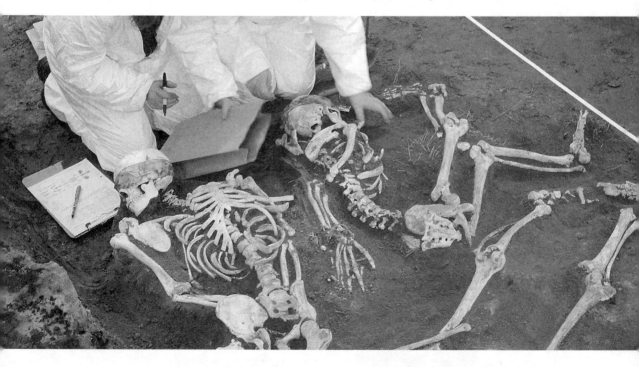

of the pelvis usually has a visible groove in the bone from each time a woman has given birth.

How Old? How Tall?

Like teeth, bones contain information about the age of the person. In children, one of the best indicators of age is the wrist. The wrist of a baby is cartilage, and feels rubbery instead of bony. As a baby ages, the cartilage gradually becomes bone. Using a wrist X-ray, a bone detective can establish a child's age to within three or four months simply by the amount of cartilage.

Ribs, too, can show age. The place where ribs fuse to the breastbone is smooth and round when a person is young. As he or she ages, however, the bones become sharp and rough. Forensic specialists can usually estimate age accurately within eighteen months if the person was thirty or younger, and within five years up to age seventy.

There are formulas for determining the height of the person as well. These are based on the long bones, those of the arms or legs. The length of the upper arm bone, or humerus, can be multiplied by five to give the approximate height of the person.

A Medical Record

Examining skeletal remains can provide a medical history of the person, too. "We always take an X-ray [of the remains], that can tell us a great deal," says McGee. "If someone has had a shoulder replacement, had an orthopedic appliance or hip replacement or something like that, it will show up on the X-ray."[27]

According to Maples, there are a surprising number of things in people's bodies that have resulted from advances in medical (and dental) technology. "Surgical procedures leave all kinds of footprints," he says. "After surgery to remove a gall bladder or a kidney, after [coronary] bypass surgery, after a mastectomy, the

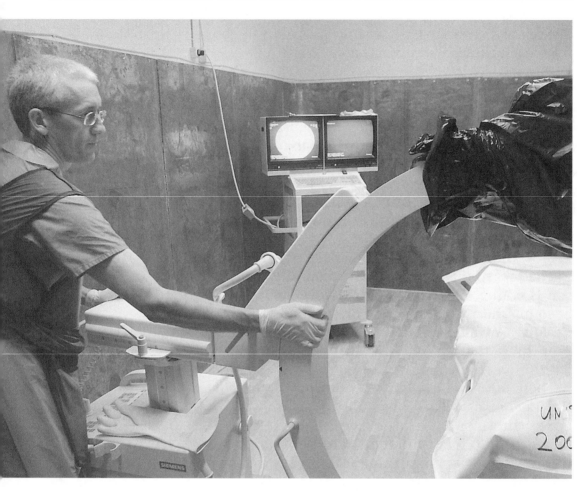

In 2002 a forensics specialist x-rays a bag filled with human remains in order to identify victims of the war in Kosovo.

blood vessels are clamped off with small metal clips. Because these clips are supposed to remain behind in the body, they are made of tough, rare metals that will resist corrosion."[28] Careful gathering of the remains may find some of these clips, and give bone detectives another clue that might help establish the person's identity.

In addition to surgical and medical procedures, skeletal remains also may explain the manner of the person's death. Forensic anthropologists have examined skulls from the Middle Ages and have identified fatal blows from clubs and spears. Similarly, ribs can show gashes from the blade of a knife, indicating that a person was stabbed.

The Colorado Cannibal

The case of a Colorado man named Alfred Packer was more than a century old when forensic anthropologists provided key evidence. Packer and his five companions were prospectors in 1874 when an early winter—frigid temperatures and blizzard conditions—forced them to hole up deep in the Colorado mountains.

When the spring thaw arrived, only Packer returned, according to one historian, "looking suspiciously well-fed."[29] Packer finally admitted that he had eaten the five men, but insisted that he had killed only one of them—and that act, he claimed, was in self-defense. He insisted that the other four had died from hunger or, in one case, had been killed by one of the other five.

In 1989 forensic anthropology professor Mames Starrs from George Washington University put together a team of experts to search for the skeletal remains of the victims and see whether they could solve the case. They found skeletal remains of the five men, and in their examination they found marks on the bones. It was clear that the skulls bore the marks of beating, and there were also marks on the bones of the hands and arms. These were explained by the experts as probable defensive wounds—the men had tried unsuccessfully to fend off hatchet blows with their arms.

The bones also showed signs that after they were dead, the men had been defleshed with a sharp knife. Starrs had seen enough to convince him that the evidence was conclusive: "Packer was as guilty as sin," he announced, "and his sins were all mortal ones."[30]

Artistic Bone Detectives

Occasionally, even after remains are examined by forensic pathologists, there is not enough data for an identification. This is especially troubling when there is evidence that the person was the victim of a crime, as in a 1987 case in Farmington, Missouri. A skull and other bones were found on the grounds of a Boy Scout camp. There was also some tattered clothing and a plastic shopping bag, which told investigators that the remains were rather recent. Police were puzzled and asked forensic pathologists for help.

They determined that the bones had belonged to a woman who was about five feet tall. From the pelvis, they could tell that she had given birth to two children. Based on the condition of her teeth, she was about twenty-five years old at the time of

"Miss Nobody"

One of the most famous facial reconstruction artists is Richard Neave, of Manchester University in Britain. In Brian Innes' book *Bodies of Evidence: The Fascinating World of Forensic Science and How It Helped Solve More than 100 True Crimes,* Innes discusses how Neave's ability to put a face on an anonymous skeleton solved a murder.

In 1989, building workers in Cardiff, south Wales, discovered a skeleton wrapped in a carpet. Pathologists . . . established that it was that of a young girl, aged fifteen, who had been buried at some time between 1981 and 1984. But what the police wanted was the face of the victim, whom they named "Miss Nobody."

Richard Neave spent two days over his reconstruction. . . . Photographs of Neave's work were distributed to the press and television, and just two days later a social worker reported that they resembled a Karen Price. Price's dental records were found and confirmed the identification. Finally, DNA extracted from the bones of the victim was compared with that from the blood of Price's parents, and the identification was complete.

The police soon uncovered Price's unhappy history. A runaway, she had taken to prostitution and, when she had refused to pose for pornographic photos, her pimp and a doorman from a local bar had killed her in a rage. Both were found guilty in February 1991.

her death. A button found at the scene was from a brand of blue jeans sold only in countries in East Asia, so the examiners decided that perhaps the woman was Asian. They also discovered what they believed was the cause of death: There was a small fracture on the back of the skull that indicated she had been struck on the head shortly before she died.

What frustrated investigators was that no one fitting the mystery woman's description had been reported missing. The bone detectives decided to try to reconstruct the woman's face from the skull outward. It was a time-consuming project, but investigators were determined to identify her, especially because it appeared she had been murdered. Perhaps a sculpted likeness might jog someone's memory.

Pegs and Clay

The first step was to make a plaster facsimile of the skull so that the original could be returned to its evidence drawer. A forensic sculptor made a mold of latex and then poured plaster into the mold. When it dried, the duplicate skull was ready to sculpt.

The sculptor cut more than two dozen rubber pegs of various lengths. These pegs represented the depth of the soft tissue atop the skull. The soft tissue—skin, muscle, and fat—lies in different thicknesses on the skull. There is more on the cheeks than along the temple, where the skin is very tight to the bone. The thicknesses differ for women and men and for various age groups.

The pegs were glued to the skull and then connected with narrow strips of modeling clay. After the pegs were connected with clay, the sculptor filled in the blank spots between the strips, and the image began to look less like a skull and more like a human face. As the sculptor worked, investigators could clearly see the high cheekbones and wide face of the mysterious woman. After adding a black wig and

A forensic artist re-creates the face of a murder victim. Such re-creations have helped law enforcement agencies to solve a number of homicides.

plastic brown eyes to the bust, they were ready to photograph it and display it on television.

A Mystery Solved

It took only three days before investigators had an answer. Several people recognized the likeness as a Thai woman named Bun Chee Nyhuis. She was married, and as far as her friends knew, she had left her husband, Richard Nyhuis, and children when she returned to Thailand several years before.

Her husband insisted that the bones could not be those of his wife. He said that he had driven her to the airport in 1983, and since she was supposedly in Thailand, he had not reported her missing. But police did not believe the story and, based on other evidence and interviews, continued to interrogate him until he confessed. He said that it had been an accident: He had pushed her and she had hit her head. That explained the skull fracture the bone detectives had found. He also admitted that he had suffocated her afterward. He said that he had buried her in the remote Boy Scout camp so that no one would know what he had done.

Richard Nyhuis was convicted of murder in 1992, and was sentenced to life in prison without parole. The crime and the victim both came to light largely because of the work of forensic anthropologists. One investigator on the case says that such results were amazing, especially because of the presence of the chilling likeness of the victim during the trial: "This is one of the few times a prosecutor got to try a murder case where the victim was actually in the courtroom with him, 'speaking' to the jury."[31]

Chapter 3

Crime Solving Through Chemistry

It may surprise people that of all the aspects of forensic science, chemistry is one of the most useful. "The guys in the lab can establish whether a homicide was the result of poison, or if a woman was drugged before she was raped," says one police officer. "They can tell you whether an athlete was on steroids when he showed up for training camp, or if someone overdosed on heroin.

"One of the reasons everyone depends on this kind of information is that it is science," he continues. "It's measurable—Victim X had such and such drug in his system when he died—and that is a fact. It doesn't depend on witnesses or an investigator's intuition or hunches. It's hard evidence, it's numbers, and in court, that kind of information is compelling."[32]

Garden-Variety Chemistry

One of the most commonly used forensic chemistry tools is carried by police and highway patrol officers to measure the presence of alcohol in a driver's bloodstream. Called the Breathalyzer, this instrument gives police a tool to confirm whether or not someone they pull over is driving under the influence of alcohol. All states have a predetermined amount of alcohol in the bloodstream that is considered illegal—usually .08 grams in every 100 milliliters of blood. And while some people have impaired driving skills at a much lower percentage, notes forensic expert D.P. Lyle, "At .08 they'll cuff you."[33]

The Breathalyzer is convenient because it measures alcohol in the bloodstream without the suspect having to give up a drop of blood. Scientists know that the level of blood-alcohol is the same as the level of alcohol in a person's exhaled breath. All that

A suspected drunk driver is given a Breathalyzer test to measure the amount of alcohol in his blood.

is needed is for the suspect to blow into the mouth-piece of the instrument. The breath goes from the mouthpiece to a small collection chamber.

When the police officer turns a switch on the Breathalyzer, the breath is immediately exposed to potassium chloride and other chemicals. The level of the potassium chloride goes down in relation to the alcohol content of the breath. The more alcohol in the breath sample, the more the potassium chloride is destroyed in the chamber.

Identifying Arson

Sometimes the substance in question is not one found in a bloodstream but one found at the scene of a crime. Arson, for example, is a serious crime in which someone purposely starts a fire. In almost every case, the arsonist uses chemicals either to start the blaze or to make sure the fire burns out of control more quickly. "The [chemicals are] called accel-

An investigator searches for evidence of chemicals to help determine whether this apartment-complex fire was an act of arson.

erants, for a good reason," says one forensic chemist, "because they really speed up the fire. Accelerants can be anything from lighter fluid to gasoline or kerosene."[34]

Sometimes firefighters suspect that accelerants were used because of the color of the flames or smoke. In most accidental fires, flames are yellow or red, and the smoke is gray or even brown. If gasoline is used, however, the flames will be whiter, and the smoke light yellow.

After the fire is extinguished, investigators gather samples of flooring or other material from the location where the fire started. They place bits of that material in clean metal cans, like paint cans. Back in the crime lab, technicians use sensitive instruments that can detect any chemical in the sample, including accelerants. If an accelerant is detected, fire marshals can say that the fire was definitely a crime—rather than an accident—and the arson squad can begin a criminal investigation.

"A Million-Piece Jigsaw Puzzle"

The most critical—and most difficult—cases for forensic chemists are those in which one or more victims die because of some poisonous substance. The difficulty lies in the fact that there are so many toxic substances available today. Poisons are everywhere—from shampoo to oven cleaner. Some seemingly harmless substances, such as vitamin D, for example, can cause severe kidney damage and therefore, in some instances, can be toxic. In many situations, finding the trace of that substance can be, as researcher David Fisher found, "like searching through a million-piece jigsaw puzzle to find the one piece that doesn't belong."[35]

Causing someone's death by toxins is certainly not a new phenomenon. In fact, murders by poison were very common in the past, largely because the crime was virtually impossible to prove unless one was caught in the act of adding a deadly substance to an enemy's food or wine. Two of the most famous poisoners were actually a pope, Alexander VI, and his son Cesare Borgia, who together murdered a large number of people as a means of gaining land and wealth. Alexander appointed wealthy men to high church offices and allowed them to continue building their fortunes. Eventually, one of the men would be invited to dinner, where the food was laced with arsenic or another type of toxin. Since the victim was a man of the church, his wealth would automatically be transferred to the pope and the church upon his death. Writes one essayist, "The Borgias selected and laid down rare poisons in their cellars with as much thought as they gave their vintage wines. Though you would often in the 15th century have heard the snobbish Roman say . . . 'I am dining with the Borgias tonight,' no Roman ever was able to say, 'I dined last night with the Borgias.'"[36]

A Range of Instruments

The Borgias would have had a much more difficult time carrying out their poisonings today, however. In fact, since the mid-nineteenth century, scientists have known that there are physical signs of poison in the body of a victim, in the blood, urine, tissues, and even the hair and fingernails.

Arsenic, a very common poison throughout history (and a favorite of the Borgias), was determined to be the cause of Napoléon Bonaparte's death as a result of modern tests on a lock of his hair. The former French emperor was defeated at Waterloo and exiled to the island of Elba. There, he began experiencing stomach problems. In his letters, he wrote of his illness, insisting that he was being poisoned by his British captors. "I am dying before my time," he wrote just a few months before his death, "murdered by the English oligarchy and its hired assassins."[37]

Questions for Two Eminent Examiners

In the May 2005 *National Geographic* article titled "In the Morgue with Al and Marcella," medical examiner Marcella Fierro and toxicologist Alphonse Poklis discuss poisoning and their roles when such a case is suspected.

[Fierro]: I take umpteen tissue samples at autopsy: heart, liver, lungs, brain, spleen, hair, nails. Blood tells you what was going on in the body at the time of death. Vitreous humor [a clear liquid] from the eye is great. It's clean. No fermentation or contamination from bacteria. Al [Alphonse Poklis] and I work together. What poisons are candidates? What's best to collect? You have to have a strategy. We'd want to know what poison the defendant would have access to. If it's a farmer, we look for agricultural things like pesticides and herbicides. We need to have an idea of where we are going. We can easily run out of tissue and blood samples before we run out of tests to do.

[Poklis]: The poisoner tries to cover up what he does, as opposed to somebody who shoots, strangles, or rapes you. A forensic psychologist I know calls poisoners custodial killers. Often you are dealing with a family situation. It happens over a period of months or a year. The perpetrator is taking care of the victim, watching him die. Poison is the weapon of controlling, sneaky people with no conscience, no sorrow, no remorse. They are scary, manipulative; if you weren't convinced by the evidence, you wouldn't believe they could do such a thing.

When he died, there were rumors that his clothes and hair showed obvious evidence of arsenic, but there was never a way of proving that he had been poisoned. However, one of his servants sealed a lock of Napoleon's hair in an envelope as a remembrance, and the envelope was passed down through generations of the valet's family.

Ben Weider, a historian and founder of the International Napoleonic Society, learned that scientists could test hair for the presence of heavy metals in the body, such as arsenic, lead, and other toxins. Weider had the hair sample tested at a prestigious European toxicology laboratory that used state-of-the-art equipment that can detect minute traces of many known toxins, including arsenic.

The laboratory results were conclusive. Even though the hair was 174 years old, it showed exposure to heavy amounts of arsenic—amounts far higher than simple environmental exposure might produce. "The poisoning of Napoleon was planned and deliberate," Weider announced. "Anything else is hogwash."[38]

"From Micrograms to Nanograms"

The confusion and inability of doctors to prove a case of poisoning is largely a thing of the past. Today, in addition to testing a victim's hair, tests can be run on blood, urine, and tissue samples from various parts of the body.

In the past, scientists looking for poisons or drugs in such samples were limited to searching for evidence visible with a microscope. Today, however, there are several tools of the trade that crime labs depend on. They are so sensitive that they can detect traces of substances that could never be detected with a microscope.

Alphonse Poklis, a Virginia toxicologist, says that the sensitivity of the instruments at his disposal has changed incredibly, as has the amount of blood or other tissue samples required for testing. "In the 1960s it took 25 milliliters of blood to detect morphine," he says. "Today we can use one milliliter to do the same work. In terms of sensitivity, we've gone from micrograms to nanograms, which is parts per billion, to parts per trillion."[39]

The Mass Spectrometer

The workhorse of the toxicology lab is the mass spectrometer. This device separates substances into their various components. There are roughly 10 million known organic chemicals, and because each of those chemicals can combine with one or more other chemicals, the number of mixtures is almost infinite. "Testing for every possible toxin, every chemical, would take forever," says one forensic scientist. "The mass spectrometer makes the job infinitely quicker."[40]

The mass spectrometer works on the principle that no two compounds have the same molecular "fingerprint," or makeup. To find a compound's finger-print, the mass spectrometer bombards it with a stream of tiny particles called electrons. The electron stream breaks the compound into fragments. By examining the pattern of fragmentation, technicians can identify the various components.

"The pattern that the mass spectrometer creates can be run through our lab's database," says forensic expert Dave Tebow, "and matched with 100 percent accuracy to a component."[41] By comparing the molecular fingerprint to the fingerprints of other known drugs or poisons, toxicologists can then do more specific tests for that substance, hopefully learning how much of the toxin is evident and how or when it was administered.

Machines Are Limited

One of the important tasks of a toxicologist is to validate the information received from the instruments

A forensic scientist uses a mass spectrometer to identify chemicals present in a human tissue sample.

Death by Toxins

Name of Toxin/Poison	What It Is	Symptoms Prior to Death	Clues Left Behind for Toxicologists
Arsenic	A heavy metal; ingested through food or drink.	Serious stomach problems, including nausea, diarrhea, and vomiting. Burning sensation in throat, cold sweats, convulsions, coma.	Buildup is easily detected in body tissue, especially nails and hair. Experts can tell how long a victim has been fed the poison by the amounts of arsenic in the roots versus the tips of the hair.
Atropine	A colorless solid chemical taken from the deadly nightshade (Atropa belladonna) plant; ingested through food or drink.	Affects nervous system and muscle cells (including heart muscles). Dilated pupils, dry mouth, fever, confusion, increased heart rate.	Presence can be detected in blood, urine, or body tissue by screening with a mass spectrometer and/or gas chromatography machine.
Carbon Monoxide	A clear, odorless gas produced from burning carbon-based fuels like gasoline; inhaled.	Victim cannot get enough oxygen when too much carbon monoxide is present. Causes drowsiness, headache, suffocation.	Gas is detected in blood through gas chromatography. When a body is found in a burned home or car—and with low carbon monoxide levels in the blood—it proves the victim did not inhale smoke but was killed before being placed in the fire.
Cyanide	Powder ingested through food or drink, or as gas inhaled or absorbed through skin.	Removes an enzyme from the body which is essential for obtaining oxygen from the blood. Causes nausea, dizziness, unconsciousness.	Victim's body tissue or breath may smell like bitter almonds. Presence can be detected in blood, urine, or body tissue by screening with a mass spectrometer and/or gas chromatography machine.
Strychnine	A colorless powder taken from the seeds of the Strychnos nux-vomica plant; ingested through food or drink.	Muscles violently contract and become very rigid, causing convulsions and asphyxiation.	Presence can be detected in blood, urine, or body tissue by screening with a mass spectrometer and/or gas chromatography machine.

and machines. Pennsylvania forensic toxicologist Frederick Fochtman notes that while analytical results cannot be disputed, they also require human interpretation.

One such case occurred when Fochtman was asked to do a drug-screening test on a worker who had been involved in a minor traffic accident. The policy of the company was that any accident, no matter how insignificant, required such a screening. In this case, the worker tested positive for the drug morphine.

"I studied the case and noted that the driver claimed to have eaten almost all of a box of crackers before reporting for work," Fochtman recalls. "The crackers in question had poppy seed baked into them, and poppies are the source of morphine, so I arranged an experiment where I asked volunteers to eat the same crackers, and I collected their urine afterward [for analysis]."[42]

The experiment found the same positive results for morphine. The worker was off the hook, says Fochtman, but he urged that in the future, screening should be designed to be more specific so that false positives would not be a problem.

Cyanide Poisoning in Seattle

Sometimes toxicology not only identifies a drug or poison but uncovers evidence leading to an arrest. One of the strangest cases involving the FBI's toxicology lab occurred in 1986, when a forty-year-old Seattle woman named Sue Snow died moments after taking two capsules of Extra-Strength Excedrin.

During the autopsy, the medical examiner detected a smell like bitter almonds, usually a sign of cyanide, a highly poisonous substance. When samples of Snow's blood and tissues were screened by toxicologists, they found evidence that she had died of cyanide poisoning. After checking her medicine cabinet for the remaining capsules in the Excedrin bottle, investigators found eight other capsules that had been laced with cyanide.

Fearing a situation of product tampering on a national scale, health officials urged consumers to stop taking any Excedrin capsules until further notice. The product was quickly removed from supermarket and pharmacy shelves, too. FBI technicians x-rayed more than 700,000 capsules and found two more poisoned bottles.

Mysterious Green Specks

Within days, a second victim was identified. Stella Nickell said that her husband, Bruce, had died just two weeks earlier after taking Extra-Strength Excedrin capsules. He had been ill with emphysema, and doctors assumed that this disease was the cause of death. The police found two more poisoned bottles in Nickell's home.

Roger Martz, the FBI toxicologist, recalls finding something odd about all the capsules that had been poisoned. "I immediately noticed several small specks of a green material that didn't seem to belong there," he says. "I found those specks in all five bottles. Identifying the cyanide was basic chemistry, and there was no way to trace it to a source. But these green specks were unique. I wondered what they were, I wondered what they were doing there, and I wondered what they might tell us about the killer."[43]

Martz ran the specks through the mass spectrometer and found that they were made up of four chemicals that were used in herbicides. He searched stores, looking at every herbicide product he could find, but none contained all four of the chemicals. Finally, he found a product that was designed to kill algae in fish tanks, and that was the one. "And there were my four chemicals," he says. "I opened up the package, and it was full of green tablets identical in color to my specks."[44]

All for Money

While the lab focused on how the specks got into Excedrin capsules, agents were concentrating on Stella Nickell. She had taken a large insurance policy out on her husband that paid only if he died from an accident (the policy included poisoning as an accident). But she had not been able to collect money at the time, since doctors had quickly ruled that emphysema had killed him. Now, with Sue Snow's death opening the case, Nickell stood to become wealthy. Could Stella Nickell be the poisoner? Could the money from an insurance policy be the motive for two deaths?

Another piece of evidence surfaced when agents remembered seeing a large aquarium in Nickell's

Trying to Poison a Judge

In 1987 a former New York University professor, John Buettner-Janusch, pleaded guilty to attempting to poison a judge. The judge, Charles L. Brieant, chief justice of the U.S. District Court in Manhattan, had sentenced him to five years in prison in 1980 for selling LSD that he had made in his college laboratory.

Buettner-Janusch bought an expensive box of candy and filled the pieces with atropine, a chemical that dramatically speeds up the heart rate. He then sent the candy to the Brieants' home, where the judge's wife sampled several pieces. Brieant discovered her unconscious on the floor when he returned from court, but fortunately, hospital staff were able to save her life.

Toxicologists from the FBI became involved in the case. Using a mass spectrometer, the team soon identified the chemical as atropine. Buettner-Janusch was arrested after forensic agents found his fingerprint on the box. When agents visited his home, they found other boxes of the expensive candy as well as the equipment he needed to poison it. Another box of candy had already been sent to his former colleague, which earned Buettner-Janusch a second count of attempted murder.

home. The most important discovery was when a fish-store employee remembered selling the woman a mortar and pestle to grind up the hard green tablets. Toxicologists realized she had used the same mortar and pestle to prepare the poison that killed her husband and Sue Snow, and the presence of the green specks in the cyanide could prove it.

"This Was an Act of Poisoning or Bioterrorism"

Toxicologists are especially gratified when they are able to identify a deadly poison before it claims a victim. That happened to Ukrainian presidential candidate Viktor Yushchenko, who was running for president against Viktor Yanukovych, the candidate backed by the Russian government. Yushchenko began experiencing severe stomach cramps and back pain in September 2004. His doctors at first thought he had a virus, but they became alarmed when his symptoms became so acute that he was in constant pain.

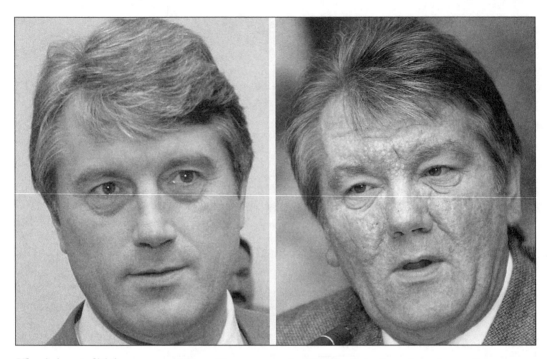

Ukrainian politician Viktor Yushchenko's photos before (left) and after (right) he was poisoned in 2004. A forensic team was able to discover the toxin used to poison him.

After three weeks Yushchenko developed a more startling symptom—large numbers of welts and cysts that distorted and disfigured his face. His doctors then suspected poison, but blood tests proved unsuccessful at identifying any known toxins. One of his physicians believed that the toxins were there but their instruments simply were not sensitive enough to detect them.

Michael Zimpfer, the head of the clinic that was treating Yushchenko, realized he needed outside help. "We were able to stabilize him, but we just didn't like how the case fit together," Zimpfer recalls. "So we gave a written document to the patient saying we had the feeling that this was an act of poisoning or bioterrorism and asked permission to get international help."[45]

In mid-December 2004 a team of toxicologists from the United States and the Netherlands became involved in the search for the mysterious toxin. Using newly developed blood tests that were more specific than any tests previously used, they found extraordinarily high levels of an environmental pollutant called dioxin—more than one thousand times the levels found in someone merely breathing polluted air. Dioxin, a by-product of the manufacturing of herbicides and paper, is extremely poisonous in such large amounts, but medical experts had not seen it used as a poison before.

Although the source of the dioxin could not be determined in the laboratory, toxicologists found that it had been administered by mouth, most likely in a liquid such as soup. The fact that such a toxin was involved in such a large quantity gave Ukrainian officials proof that it was a case of intentional poisoning—a criminal case.

Chapter 4

Questioned Documents

Paper plays a dominant role in a surprising number of crimes. Whether it is a check with a signature that does not look right, a kidnapper's ransom note, or an old manuscript that a dealer claims was written during the Civil War, people have a strong interest in validating paper. When such paper is connected with a crime—or if it is a forgery that is being passed off as genuine—forensic scientists are often called on to evaluate what is called a "questioned document," or QD.

"What a Genius"

Evaluating ink is one way to find out when a questioned document was written. Inks vary not only by color but by chemical makeup. According to one retired police officer, however, some QDs need no more than a little common sense to evaluate.

"Sometimes you can't believe how stupid some people are," he says. "My rookie year as a police officer a woman came in screaming because she had written a check to her boyfriend for $30. She found out that he had cashed it, but somewhere between the time she wrote the check and he cashed it, the amount changed to $3,000.

"She said that he'd changed the amount, adding the extra zeroes. But the guy hadn't even bothered to use the same color ink. She had written the check with a ballpoint pen in black ink. What a genius—he added the zeroes in turquoise ink, probably a felt-tip pen. I don't know who was more confused, the boyfriend or the person who cashed such a goofy-looking check."[46]

A forensic document examiner uses a powerful microscope to verify the authenticity of a signature.

The Ink of the Vinland Map

The U.S. Secret Service, which watches for counterfeit currency, maintains the largest ink database in the world. Called the International Ink Library, it contains the chemical compositions of more than seven thousand different inks, both modern and historical. When a QD's ink is being examined, scientists can get the information they need from this database.

One QD case in which ink analysis has been important is that of the Vinland map. Discovered in 1950, the map is believed by many to have been created in 1440. It depicts Viking exploration of parts of the New World. If the map is genuine, it is proof that the Vikings were ahead of Christopher Columbus in exploring the New World.

The first analysis of the map was promising. Tests run on the parchment itself established that it was certainly old enough to be genuine. It was the analysis of the ink, however, that proved to be a stumbling block for many scientists. Researchers at University College in London used a spectrometer with a laser that could break down the ink into its chemical components.

They found that the ink contained a chemical called anatase, which has never been found as a component of other medieval inks. As far as ink specialists know, anatase was not used in inks until after World War I. Many historians believe that the test results are proof that the Vinland map is a fake, although they admit that the genuine parchment gives them pause. But anthropologist Kenneth L. Feder says, "Someone could have been real bright about it and got themselves an old piece of parchment." After all, he says, "if you were going to fake such a map, you wouldn't go out to the local Staples to get a piece of paper."[47]

Paper and the Hitler Diaries

Paper, like ink, can also be examined for hints of the document's authenticity. Most paper is made from

wood fibers and cotton, and sometimes synthetic or natural components are added to give it color or durability. There are also ingredients that make paper less absorbent so that ink appears sharp and clear. Some paper—especially fine stationery—has a watermark, which is a translucent design that can be seen by holding the paper up to the light. The design is impressed on the paper during manufacture. All of these things can help investigators determine how recently the paper was made. In the case of "Hitler's Secret Diaries" that surfaced in 1982, the ability of scientists to date paper was all that was needed to prove that the documents were a fraud.

A reporter from Germany's *Stern* magazine had excitedly called his editors with the news that a large number of notebooks kept as diaries by Adolf Hitler had come into his hands. If the diaries were real, it was amazing news, for all of Hitler's personal papers were reportedly destroyed in a plane crash during the last days of World War II. *Stern* editors agreed to

Konrad Kujau holds up notebooks he claimed were Hitler's diaries. Forensic experts, however, concluded his documents were little more than forgeries.

pay the $3.8 million to publish the diaries and sell them to other magazines around the world, including some in the United States.

Skeptical historians urged that *Stern* have the diaries authenticated by experts before they were published. The magazine agreed, and in 1983 forensic examiners from the United States and Switzerland inspected the documents. It was quickly determined that they were forgeries. As one expert said disdainfully, "They are not only forgeries, they are bad forgeries."[48]

The forger, a forty-six-year-old German man named Konrad Kujau, failed on a number of levels, but the most obvious was the choice of paper. Spectrometry and the use of ultraviolet light on the diaries' paper showed that it contained a whitening agent (to make the paper brighter) that had not even been developed until the mid-1950s. In addition, the bindings of the diaries contained polyester, which also had not been developed until years after World War II. On the basis of such tests, the case against Kujau was airtight, and he was sent to prison.

Machines Can Talk

Forensic examiners say that they can get a great deal of evidence from the machines used to create documents, too. There have been cases in which a specific typewriter has been identified as the source of a ransom note or a piece of hate mail simply because of its slight imperfections.

In one 1987 case in a suburb of Chicago, a woman claimed that she was receiving threatening letters from a man who lived across the street. He denied leaving her the letters, and police were called. Investigators knew that the woman had a history of making accusations, especially against black members of the community. They wanted to be sure that she was not falsely accusing her neighbor because he was black.

The case was solved quickly. The notes were written on an older-model typewriter with several broken type bars. The capital letter *Y* had a nick each time it was used. The man did not own a typewriter, nor did he have access to one at work. An old Royal machine was found in the back bedroom of the woman's house, and tests showed that the letter *Y* was broken. She had been writing the hateful letters herself, hoping to cause trouble for her neighbor.

Copy Machines and Banana Peels

Identifiable imperfections are not limited to old-fashioned machines like typewriters. Often the most modern copiers and laser printers can have "signatures," too. "People believe photocopiers are not traceable, and that's just not true," says one QD analyst. "With a little luck, we can not only prove a document was made on a specific machine, we can determine within a narrow period of time when it was made."[49]

Questioned documents can sometimes be matched to a specific copy machine or laser printer because of the pattern of what are called trash marks. On a laser printer, for instance, the light-sensitive drum accumulates dirt as well as tiny fissures and tear marks. These appear as tiny black dots that will be in the same formation on every page that is printed. Photocopiers, too, record every mark and scratch on the machine's glass.

The imperfections on a photocopier's glass helped police arrest a terrorist in Miami in the late 1980s. Calling himself "El Condor," he had set off bombs near the walls of several federal buildings throughout the city. Before each bombing, El Condor sent notes, but rather than an original document, each was a photocopy. Unfortunately for investigators, the copies showed different imperfections each time. It seemed clear that El Condor did not own a copy machine but probably used coin-operated machines in public places.

After another bombing, FBI agents searched the surrounding neighborhood, comparing the note to

The Sad Case of Peter Weinberger

In 1956 a month-old baby named Peter Weinberger was kidnapped from the patio of his New York home. Near his empty baby carriage lay a hastily scrawled ransom note written in green ink. The kidnapper, who signed the note "Your baby sitter," demanded $2,000 and urged the parents to pay or the child would be killed.

Investigators had few clues, so they concentrated on the note itself. They noted several idiosyncrasies in the handwriting, especially the formation of the letter *m*, which looked more like a sideways letter *z*, and the exaggerated loop on certain capital letters. There were no computers in those days, and when examiners decided to look through public documents hoping to spot a match, it was done totally by hand.

They searched as many local records in New York as they could find—licenses, registration forms, hospital records, and post office files. Whenever one of the examiners found a sample of writing that seemed similar, it was given to agents to investigate further.

Finally—seven weeks and 2 million documents later—an agent (one of hundreds involved in the search) found a match on a probation violation form filled out by a thirty-one-year-old man named Angelo LaMarca, who had been arrested for bootlegging. When agents confronted LaMarca, he promptly confessed and led them to the baby's body. He was given the death penalty for his crime.

coin-operated machines at convenience stores and libraries. At one store, they found a piece of a banana peel wedged in the rubber cover of the copy machine. That matched a dark stain found on the most recent note. By interviewing employees at the store, they were able to get a description of the suspect who used the machine, which eventually led to his arrest.

Suicide or Murder?

Far easier than comparing typewriters and photocopiers is examining a person's handwriting. This can be important in verifying the validity of a handwritten will, for example, or whether a check was endorsed by the person to whom it was written. Sometimes, the task is more grim, as Boston police found when they investigated a 2003 case in which a man was found hanging in his basement. A suicide note was discovered on his workbench, just a few feet from where he died.

Though the man's family was devastated by the death, they were not completely surprised. He had suffered from clinical depression for years, and had mentioned suicide more than once. After reading the note, the man's wife insisted that he had not written it. The note had been printed by hand and she said that her husband used only cursive, never printing when he wrote.

After testing the note for fingerprints, it appeared she was right. There were several fingerprints on the note, but none matched those of her husband. A subsequent investigation finally found that he had been murdered, and his former business partner was charged with the crime. He had not tried to imitate the victim's handwriting, believing that, because of the man's bouts with depression, the family would be convinced that his death was a suicide.

Looking at Hauptman's Handwriting

Document examiners who specialize in handwriting say that their job is far different from that of the graphologist, a person who analyzes handwriting to determine personality type. Document examiners are interested only in the physical aspects of the writings. They determine, for example, whether the writing in an anonymous letter (such as a ransom note) matches the handwriting of a suspect.

One of the first cases in which handwriting analysis proved valuable involved one of the most famous crimes of the twentieth century—the kidnapping of aviator Charles Lindbergh's two-year-old son. After the child was kidnapped, the Lindberghs received a ransom note demanding a payment of $50,000. Although the ransom was paid, the child was not returned. Two months after the kidnapping, the child's body was found in a nearby woods. Two and a half years later, a German carpenter named Bruno

Hauptman was caught with some of the ransom money in his possession.

One of the first things investigators were interested in was whether Hauptman was the author of the handwritten ransom note. Hauptman voluntarily provided handwriting samples after his arrest, and analysts compared those to the note. The unusual way the capital H's were formed, as well as the shape and spacing of the other letters, convinced examiners that Hauptman had written the ransom note. On the basis of this and other evidence, he was convicted of the crime and sent to the electric chair in 1936.

Forged Signatures

Handwriting analysts look at a number of things in a sample. In a sample that includes a possibly forged

A writing expert compares the handwriting of Bruno Hauptman with ransom notes from the Lindbergh kidnapping. This forensic evidence helped convict Hauptman of the crime.

signature, they look for microscopic signs of pencil marks, indicating that the forger lightly traced the signature before going over it in ink. They also look for evidence of erasures, which would not be there in an authentic signature.

One of the most common ways that forgers give themselves away is by lifting the pen off the paper during the signature process. People sign their own names in a fluid motion, but a person who is copying someone else's signature goes slowly, stopping and starting as they compare what they are doing to a real signature. Sometimes called "forger's tremors," those hesitations are obvious under magnification.

Another common error made by forgers is trying to make a signature an exact replica of an original. Experts say that people rarely sign their names exactly the same way twice. Whether a person is tired, stressed, ill, or even using a different pen than normal, his or her signature varies slightly each time. In fact, a perfect match between signatures raises red flags for investigators, leading them to suspect that the image was traced.

A final common mistake that forgers make is focusing only on the shape of the letters, rather than the upward or downward movement of the signature. For example Abraham Lincoln's signature varied in some ways but always showed an upward progression from the capital *A* to the first four letters of the last name, and another climb for the last two letters, the *l* and the *n*. Many forgers of Lincoln's signature failed because they did not notice the upward climb of his signature each time he signed his name.

Looking for Internal Inconsistencies

Not all criminals try to replicate someone else's handwriting. Sometimes they do just the opposite— try to disguise their writing so it cannot be traced to them. This may occur when someone sends a ransom note or hate mail. People disguise their writing in several ways. Men will often attempt a more delicate style, trying to make their writing seem more feminine by adding flourishes or making their writing rounder and larger. Conversely, some women will try for a more masculine style—smaller and less fluid in shape. Many people will write with the opposite hand they normally use or try to make letters slant in a different direction.

Experts, however, can usually see through such tricks, because as people continue writing, they almost always revert to the writing habits they have always had. For example, a handwriting sample may start out disguised by odd slants or flourishes, but the slants and flourishes become more scarce and less pronounced throughout the sample. The longer a person writes, the more the automatic aspects of handwriting begin to surface. One writing expert says that the inconsistency of a sample is often a strong clue that suspects are disguising their writing:

> Think of how odd it feels to put on your left sock first if you always put on the right one first. Or how uncomfortable you feel if you forget to put on your wristwatch. . . . When we examine an example of handwriting, we look for internal consistency. A high degree of internal consistency suggests that this is the person's normal writing habit. A high degree of inconsistency suggests attempts at disguise.[50]

Indented Writing

One sure way to prove that a suspect wrote a ransom note or forged a check is to find the origin of the writing. "It sounds farfetched, but investigators have solved cases by finding a pad of paper that shows indentions of a [ransom] note," says one forensic technician. "If you hold the paper up to the light at an angle, the impressions are there, and it's a pretty

Authentic Signatures or Forgeries?

When analyzing famous signatures for authenticity, experts look for several things. A common error made by forgers is trying to make a signature an exact replica of the original. Experts say people rarely sign their names exactly the same way twice. Note that while Abraham Lincoln's signature is similar in these first three authentic examples, it is never exactly the same.

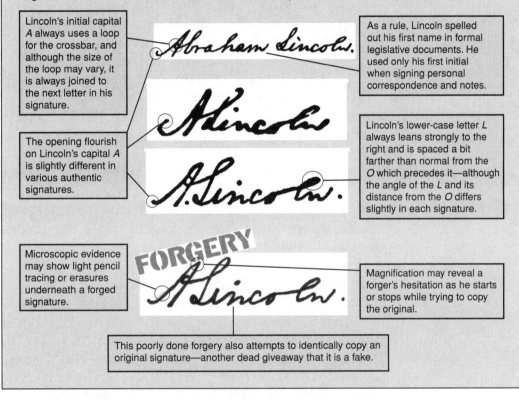

Lincoln's initial capital *A* always uses a loop for the crossbar, and although the size of the loop may vary, it is always joined to the next letter in his signature.

As a rule, Lincoln spelled out his first name in formal legislative documents. He used only his first initial when signing personal correspondence and notes.

The opening flourish on Lincoln's capital *A* is slightly different in various authentic signatures.

Lincoln's lower-case letter *L* always leans strongly to the right and is spaced a bit farther than normal from the *O* which precedes it—although the angle of the *L* and its distance from the *O* differs slightly in each signature.

Microscopic evidence may show light pencil tracing or erasures underneath a forged signature.

Magnification may reveal a forger's hesitation as he starts or stops while trying to copy the original.

This poorly done forgery also attempts to identically copy an original signature—another dead giveaway that it is a fake.

standard process to get a copy of the letter from those impressions."[51]

Such evidence has made all the difference in some crime cases. In a 1986 Massachusetts case, a woman was at the center of a murder investigation. Her boyfriend had been shot and killed on his birthday, and near his body was a letter that read, "Happy Birthday, Friend." Police suspected that the man had been killed by the woman's jealous ex-boyfriend. Investigators intended to compare the handwriting on the note with a sample of the suspect's handwriting they found in his car. It was not a large sample of writing, just an envelope with a woman's name and address written on it.

The handwriting expert recalls how luck—and the rising sun—contributed to an amazing discovery:

> I was working in an office with a window look-ing east. I was there about seven o'clock in the morning, and the envelope just happened to be lying on my desk. As the sun rose behind me, sunlight streamed into my office, and I saw that there was indented writing on it. When I looked at it more closely, I could see the indentions read, "Happy Birthday, Friend."[52]

Obviously, the presence of indentions of the killer's note on an envelope belonging to the suspect was strong proof that he had written the note—and therefore was the killer. He was convicted of murder, largely due to that evidence.

Linguistic Analysis

Occasionally it is not the physical clues of handwrit-ing that are most helpful but the essence of what is written on the page. Some experts can find clues in the style of language, the grammar, and the vocabu-

Clues Under the Paper

One of the most interesting tools used by document analysts is the electrostatic detection apparatus (ESDA). Someone writing on a pad of paper leaves an impression of that writing on the paper un-derneath. The ESDA reveals what was written on the paper above by reading the impressions.

A technician places the impressed paper on top of a metal grid that is electrically charged and pulls a thin piece of plastic—usually Mylar—across the top. Vacuum suction under the metal holds the plastic and paper together while a mixture of photocopier toner and tiny glass beads is applied. The indented parts of the paper (the impressions) become electrically charged, and as a result, the mix-ture of toner and glass beads clings to it, making it readable.

lary used in a questioned document. This type of investigation is called linguistic analysis, and it has proved very effective in recent years.

The idea behind linguistic analysis is that when people write, they display unique characteristics in their words, phrases, and grammar. These can be as individual as their handwriting. They might consistently mix up "their" and "there," for example, or use apostrophes incorrectly. They may use words or phrases that mark them as being from a certain part of the country, or that may even suggest that their first language is not English.

The latter was one of the conclusions drawn by the FBI forensic team when they studied the ransom note in the Lindbergh kidnapping case. The placement of dollar signs after an amount, for example, is used frequently in Europe but never in the United States. Also, there was almost no punctuation used, and many words were misspelled. In the note, the word *gute* was used for "good," and that suggested someone whose first language was German. When German immigrant Bruno Hauptman was caught with ransom money in his possession, the examiners felt that, on the basis of the note at least, he seemed a likely suspect.

Words of Hate

The FBI and other law enforcement agencies keep databases of text and vocabulary styles of known hate groups. When a threatening letter was sent to a white church youth group that was planning to help rebuild a black church in 2000, investigators recognized certain phrases about white supremacy as well as racial epithets. Such phrases appeared frequently in pamphlets and other literature distributed by militant groups in Virginia and West Virginia. By narrowing down the suspects to these groups, police were able to locate the individuals responsible for the threats.

Federal agents arrest Ted Kaczynski in 1996. Linguistic analysis of Kaczynski's sixty-five-page-long manifesto helped identify him as the Unabomber.

Linguistic analysis was also done on the sixty-five-page-long "Unabomber Manifesto" sent to the *New York Times* and *Washington Post* in 1995. The document mailed by the anonymous Unabomber explained his eighteen-year terrorist bombing campaign. His sixteen homemade bombs killed three people and injured twenty-nine others, and although the FBI had launched a wide investigation, it had no clues regarding the Unabomber's identity.

The analysis of the document revealed little, other than it was clear that the man was bright and well educated. It was not until the document was published in the newspapers that a woman named Linda Patrik came forward. She recognized some of the words and phrases in the manifesto: She had heard her brother-in-law use those same words.

Patrik downloaded the document and showed it to her husband, David Kaczynski, who agreed that it sounded familiar. A number of phrases stood out, but one that he had heard his brother Ted use many times was "cool-headed logicians." Says linguistic analyst Don Foster, who worked on the case, "The entire [manifesto] was structured like a badly edited academic dissertation—or like one of Ted's angry letters from Montana. . . . David did not have to study the whole 35,000 word document from beginning to end. He had heard it all before, and he recognized the voice."[53]

Soon afterward, Ted Kaczynski was arrested for the bombings, a case that might never have been solved had it not been for a family member's recognition of familiar phrases.

Chapter 5

Crime Scene Impressions

One of the fastest growing areas of forensics is concerned with the marks or impressions a criminal makes and leaves behind—which can include shoe prints, the tire marks of a car, or impressions from the tools used to gain entry into a house or to break a lock. Such impressions can reveal a surprising amount of information that can be invaluable in solving crimes.

Thousands of Tread Marks

Tire treads are a good example of a valuable forensic tool. "If you look at a bunch of cars in a parking lot, and just stare at the tires, it may seem that they're all alike," says one forensic scientist. "But they're not. They differ in width, a lot of features that tire manufacturers add to reduce noise, to make the tire last longer, to give it more stability on slippery roads, things like that. If you take a real close look, you'll see a real variety in the details."[54]

Besides being manufactured with different tread patterns, individual tires wear differently. Cars are seldom aligned perfectly, and that means that tires get wear and tear on the edges, rather than the middle. Parts of the tread become worn. Or a rock or nail

74

can become wedged in a tread and leave its mark in the tire's impression.

Because they differ, tire treads can be matched with certainty to marks found at a crime scene. Databases with thousands of tread patterns and specifications for what types of vehicles the tires are typically found on are available to law enforcement agencies.

"It helps, too, because you can find out that the tire is usually found on let's say a van or a little pickup," says one police officer. "Then you aren't wasting time by having people looking at SUVs or a VW or something. Anything to narrow it down helps."[55]

Tire Tread Tracks

Tire tread patterns can be matched to tracks found at a crime scene. Experts compare tracks with those found in tire track databases. The databases hold thousands of different tire tread patterns and specifications for what types of vehicles the tire is typically found on. Besides matching the tire track to a certain type of vehicle, tracks can hold other clues that link a specific vehicle to the crime scene.

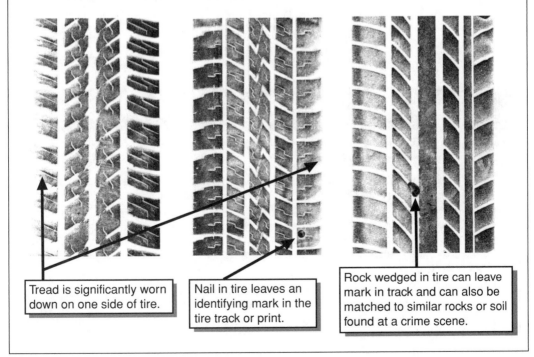

Tread is significantly worn down on one side of tire.

Nail in tire leaves an identifying mark in the tire track or print.

Rock wedged in tire can leave mark in track and can also be matched to similar rocks or soil found at a crime scene.

Being able to state with certainty that a particular tire was at a crime scene is powerful evidence, although like a fingerprint, a specific tread mark is not an indicator of guilt. Nevertheless, if a person says that his or her car could not have been in the area and forensic technicians can prove by means of tread marks that it was, it is proof that the person is not telling the truth, and the investigation can proceed from there.

Preserving Tire Marks

When tread marks are found at a crime scene, the first thing investigators notice is whether they are in a soft medium, such as soil, sand, or even snow, or if the marks are on a hard surface, such as cement or asphalt. Those on a hard surface can be seen clearly only if the vehicle has been driven through something that could make the tread pattern stand out, such as paint, oil, or a patch of mud.

In one case in Maryland, blood was the key. A woman had been killed and her body dumped from a car. After she landed on the road, the driver backed through her blood, which left partial prints of the

"We Got Nothing but a Soggy Mess"

Learning to make casts of tire or shoe tread impressions is not easy, as one forensic examiner explains in this excerpt from N.E. Genge's *The Forensic Casebook*.

"My first shoe print was a disaster," Paul Gaetan recalls. "I wasn't a print person, just winging it, but there was no one else available and I figured something—no matter how bad—was better than nothing. Even a shoe size would help, right? The print was an oily substance, but I didn't know what. I waited for it to dry a bit, then blew black powder over it and blew away the excess. The lifting material was overlapping tape that I affixed to a piece of white cardstock and shipped off to the lab down south, thinking, 'That wasn't so bad.' . . .

"The guy who opened it had me on the phone in no time, gave me an earful on my 'technique.' The 'oil' wasn't oil, exactly. It was brake fluid or something. It melted the tape and we got nothing but a soggy mess for our trouble. Thank God for photos. I think he'd have flown up and shaken me if I hadn't taken photos!

tread pattern on the cement. To preserve the evidence, the investigator ordered the forensic team to bring in chunks of the road that contained parts of the print.

One of the forensic examiners recalls that the job was a heavy one, but the results were well worth the effort. The tread pattern was documented and compared to a database of thousands of tire patterns. "Three large sections . . . were brought in by hydraulic lift," he says, "and from those we were able to enhance some faint impressions and make a positive match to her husband's car."[56]

Far more likely to help an investigation, however, are the three-dimensional impressions in a softer surface. If such an impression is found, forensic technicians make a casting of the print. First, they make a metal or wooden frame around the impression. Then they pour either plaster or a dental stone mixture into the impression and allow it to harden. The finished impression can be stored and compared with patterns of suspects' tires at a later time.

Looking for One Goodyear

One situation that can be extremely helpful in narrowing down the possible matches to a particular tire is when the tread patterns show that different types of tires were on the vehicle in question. One good example was a case in south London in 1990 in which a woman had been strangled. She had been left by the road, and tire tracks were found near the body.

The forensic examiners made impressions of the two front tires and discovered that the one on the right was a Dunlop tire and the other was a Goodyear. The victim's husband, who was a suspect because of other evidence, happened to drive a Volvo that had three Dunlop tires and a Goodyear tire on the front left. The two front tires matched the impressions, so police had good reason to believe that his car had been at the scene.

But that alone was not enough. After all, there might have been hundreds of cars with those same two kinds of tires on the road. Examiners did some research on the Goodyear tire. They found that that particular model was mostly exported to Holland, and only a very small number were sold to dealers in Britain. Of the customers in Britain who purchased that tire, only the husband of the victim had it on the front paired with a Dunlop.

The likelihood that another car, says one forensic examiner, "carrying a Dunlop on its nearside front and the particular type of Goodyear on its offside front, could have been in London on March 30 was infinitesimal."[57] Based on that and other evidence, the case against the woman's husband was airtight.

Shoe Treads

Tires are not the only tread marks found at crime scenes. Shoes, too, can provide numerous clues by their tread pattern, and there are tens of thousands of them in use today, far more than the number of tire treads. Says one examiner, "Looking at just the shoes made by the Nike and Adidas companies alone could be a full-time job."[58] As with tires, databases are kept by both manufacturers and law enforcement agencies. A clear shoe print can be identified and compared to a suspect's shoes.

A shoe print can tell investigators a number of things. First, identical styles and brands of shoes look different, depending on the wearer. People walk in different ways, and, depending on the surface they tread on, the soles of their shoes show wear in different places. "Some people walk more on the outsides of their feet," says one forensic expert, "others favor the heel, and still others shuffle along on the balls of their feet. How your foot strikes the ground determines how the sole of your shoe will wear."[59]

In addition, the tread may provide other information, such as one shoe tread that is deeper than the

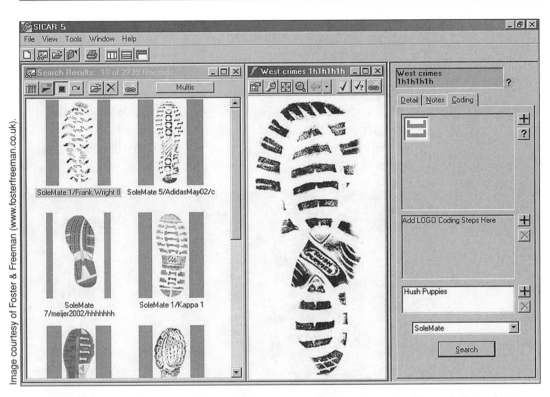

Image courtesy of Foster & Freeman (www.fosterfreeman.co.uk).

other, which signals that the wearer was limping when the prints were made. Or a stone wedged in the tread may show up in a suspect's shoe. With luck, says forensic expert John Houde, "a nick or gouge in the heel area of a print left in the mud at a murder scene may match perfectly with a pair of shoes recovered from a man's closet."[60]

Forensic investigators use a computer program to help compare the partial shoe print on the right with known brands on the left.

Snow Prints

Shoe prints at a crime scene are processed much like tire treads. If the prints are on a soft surface, a cast is made with plaster or dental stone. Shoe prints can even be processed in snow, although it is much trickier than making a cast in soil or sand. That is because snow is far more fragile, and if it melts even a little when the plaster is poured in, crucial detail is lost.

"There's a product called Snow Print Wax, which you can apply to the print, like spray paint," says one forensic examiner. "It gives it a little shell, and after you spray it, you can safely use a plaster cast."[61] Many people might think that prints in snow cannot be very helpful, but forensic snow evidence has solved some serious crimes. In one arson case, investigators noticed what looked like boot prints in the snow, but there was something very unusual about them.

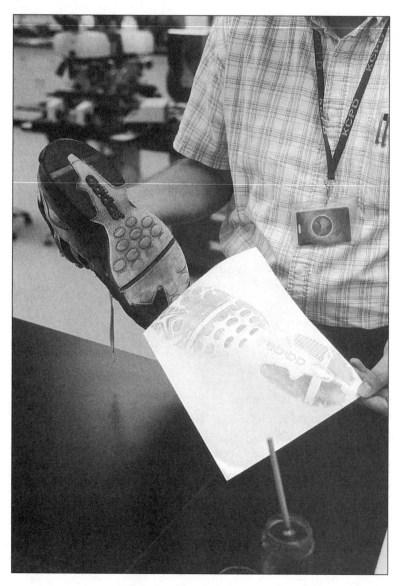

A crime lab scientist makes a print of a shoe tread on paper. The print will be compared against prints found at a crime scene.

"Every so often, there would be a little round mark on one side [of the boot print]," says forensic scientist Dave Tebow. "They made . . . casts of it all and eventually they looked at what they had and realized the little hole was a cane mark." The cane belonged to a neighbor whose daughter had been dating the man whose house had been set on fire. The father was resentful because the man had abused his daughter. "So he burned the guy's house down," Tebow says. "At first, he denied being anywhere near the scene, but because of the recent snow, and the cane marks, he was clearly lying. They solved that case because of the snow print."[62]

Latent Footprints

Just as fingerprints can be latent, shoe prints can be hidden, too. But even a clean, dry shoe can leave a mark on a countertop or a smooth floor. "I've seen cases where they get a latent print from a door somebody kicked in," says one police officer. "And another one where two guys robbed a house and then trashed what was left. One of them kicked over a television set and left a print on the screen glass."[63]

After viewing a crime scene, forensic scientists often use lasers in places likely to yield a latent shoe print. Doors are a good bet, and if the crime was murder, the area around the victim's body may have a latent print. Technicians also give large pieces of broken glass attention with the laser. After locating a latent print, technicians apply fingerprint powder and lift it with tape just as they lift a fingerprint.

"You May Never Notice It"

Helpful leads can come from the marks tools leave at a crime scene, too. Two screwdrivers may look the same, but under a microscope, the tips show variations that make them almost as unique as fingerprints.

"Sometimes it's wear and tear. Maybe a screwdriver is used for something it's not designed for," says one forensic examiner. "It gets a little nick out of the end, and while you may never notice it, we can see it under magnification. Another reason for the variation can be traced back to the manufacturer. I examined a cheap screwdriver a few months ago that had a pretty obvious defect, probably caused by an air bubble [that formed during production]. So the metal actually had a smooth round hole on the end—pretty hard to miss."[64]

When a tool mark is left at the crime scene—especially in a softer surface such as putty, wood, or caulk—the mark is first photographed. Forensic technicians then usually remove the piece of wood or window frame that shows the mark and bring it to the lab. However, if the mark is on something that cannot be moved easily, such as a front door, they make a cast of it, just as they would a shoe print or tire tread mark.

If investigators have a tool that they believe made the mark, forensic specialists use it to make the same mark in the lab. It is critical that they do not use the tool on a hard surface, for it may damage the tool and make the evidence worthless. Instead, they may use an aluminum or lead rod, neither of which would further mark the suspect's tool. The two marks—the one made in the lab and the original—are then carefully examined under a powerful compound microscope. Looking at the two marks side by side, an examiner can quickly determine whether they were made with the suspect's tool.

A Suspicious Ladder

One of the first cases in which tool marks were used as forensic evidence was the Lindbergh kidnapping. Very little evidence had been left at the scene of the crime. One of the only pieces of evidence was the homemade ladder that was used to get to the child's bedroom on the second floor of the house.

Once the suspect, Bruno Hauptman, was arrested, police found a carpenter's plane in his garage. Forensic examination of the plane showed that it produced cuts that were identical to those found on the ladder. In addition to the plane, police discovered

Teeth as Tools

Sometimes forensic examiners find clues not just in teeth but in the bite marks they leave. Ted Bundy, one of the most notorious American serial killers, was convicted partly because of his teeth marks on the body of his last victim.

When Bundy broke in to a Florida State University sorority house in January 1978, he viciously attacked four young residents, seriously injuring two of them and killing Margaret Bowman and Lisa Levy. Medical examiners found bite marks on Levy's body and took photographs so that they could be compared to the tooth marks of any suspects the police might identify.

A month after the murders, Bundy was arrested, and because police thought that he could be a suspect, forensic odontologists asked for a dental impression. They took photographs of his teeth, which were uneven and left a very unusual mark. When the photographs of the mark on Levy's body were compared with Bundy's dental impression, the two matched perfectly. Together with other evidence, that was enough to send him to prison—and eventually the electric chair.

During the 1979 murder trial of Ted Bundy, a forensic odontologist demonstrates that Bundy's bite perfectly matches bite marks found on one of the victims.

that Hauptman's attic had a missing floorboard, and examiners determined that the board had been used to construct the ladder. The sawed end of the board used in the ladder matched up perfectly to the other floorboards in the attic. The forensic examiners had made a connection between Hauptman's tools and wood and the ladder at the crime scene.

"It's Not Going to Send Anyone to Prison"

Forensic examiners say that it is important to remember that the work they do rarely proves that a person is guilty of a crime. "Lots of times on television, crime shows make it seem like all you have to do is show that a screwdriver came out of a suspect's tool chest, and he's cooked," says one investigator. "But that isn't the case at all.

"It's really very much like most fingerprint evidence. By showing that a person was present at the crime scene, fingerprint techs are only doing just that. It doesn't necessarily mean he robbed the place, or strangled the victim, or whatever the crime was. It just establishes presence. That's the same with matching up a tool mark to a person. In and of itself, it's not going to send anyone to prison."[65]

One police officer recalls finding a tip of a screwdriver on the ground at the scene of a burglary. "They processed it as evidence," he says. "It was photographed and everything. And at the time there wasn't a suspect, so they had nothing to compare it to. But later, they found a guy who they suspected. As it turned out, in his truck he had a toolbox with a screwdriver that was broken at the tip, and the two parts matched perfectly.

"The guy claimed he'd never been near that house [that had gotten burglarized]," he adds. "But that screwdriver tip placed him there. It didn't show that he did it, but it *did* show that he wasn't being truthful with the police. In this case, when they caught him in that lie, he ended up confessing."[66]

"He Tried to Outwit the Lab Guys"

Some criminals are aware of the damning evidence that tool marks can provide and have tried to take precautions against having their tools identified. One forensic expert recalls a burglar who had had a great deal of success in doing just that:

We had a guy who carried around a big channel lock wrench—a huge thing. He'd use it to literally twist off doorknobs. And he had a big screwdriver he used to open locks. They were what you call 'no-nonsense' tools for a burglar. Anyway, after he committed the burglary, he'd go home—where he had a machine shop.

The guy would then proceed to grind down the tools he'd used, so they would lose some of the identifying marks. We were curious, because there were a bunch of burglaries with the same MO [modus operandi], the same details. And they were happening in roughly the same area of the county. But we were curious, because each burglary left tool marks that didn't match with one another. Anyway, the police finally caught the guy on his way home from committing another burglary—before he'd had a chance to grind the tools down. He tried to outwit the lab guys. He almost did.[67]

Chapter 6

The DNA Fingerprint

Of all the forensic tools available, DNA evidence has become the most highly valued. It is as individual as a fingerprint, but has one distinct advantage over fingerprints. While fingerprints come only from fingers, DNA comes from everywhere on a person's body—hair, blood, semen, saliva, skin, and even tears. One U.S. associate attorney general explains, "DNA is to the 21st century what fingerprinting was to the 20th. The widespread use of DNA evidence is the future of law enforcement in this country."[68]

A Ladder with 3 Billion Rungs

DNA, short for deoxyribonucleic acid, is a molecule that is found in the nucleus of living cells in the body. It sparked a great deal of interest among geneticists in the mid-twentieth century because they believed that DNA held the coded information that was the key to understanding heredity in humans.

The DNA molecule is a complex structure with two strands connected by various chemicals, sort of like a ladder with 3 billion rungs. It is tightly wound around and around, and is often pictured as a double helix. If the single DNA molecule in a cell's nucleus were unwound, it would be nearly six feet long.

When its chemical makeup was discovered in 1953, no one envisioned its application to crime solving or other legal matters. What mattered to geneticists was its application to chemistry, biology, and, by finding the basis for certain diseases that are genetically transmitted, medicine. It was not until 1984 that a British geneticist named Alec Jeffreys found a practical application for DNA in the world of criminal justice.

British geneticist Alec Jeffreys holds the first DNA fingerprint profile in 1984. Jeffreys convinced English authorities to begin using DNA evidence to help solve crimes.

A Genetic Bar Code

Scientists knew that the pattern of the chemicals making up the rungs on the DNA ladder was important. They also knew that most of the molecule's genetic instructions—99.9 percent of them—dealt with characteristics that all humans share, a brain, two legs, a heart, and so on.

It was Jeffreys who was able to find the tiny part of the molecule that was different for each person, that explained, for instance, why someone's eyes were blue or brown, or whether that person would be prone to baldness as an adult. Jeffreys found, too, that he could isolate this part of the chain and print its pattern on a photographic plate. The result, called an autorad, looks like a blurry bar code that one might see on a package in the grocery store. Comparing an autorad of one person to that of another would be like comparing the fingerprints of two individuals.

Jeffreys believed that this could have immediate applications. It could be used as a tool to identify the true father of a child, for example. Since one strand of a person's DNA comes from the mother and the other from the father, that strand of a child's DNA would show a match to the true father and resolve paternity suits. Jeffreys also realized that if blood, semen, or skin were found at the scene of a crime, DNA could be taken from it and compared to a DNA sample from a suspect. And because only identical twins share the same DNA, the results for most people would be as specific as a fingerprint.

Testing the Idea

The first cases in which DNA analysis was used involved the rape and murder of two 15-year-old girls in the village of Narborough, England. The first occurred in 1983, and the second in 1986. Even though DNA's value at a crime scene was completely unknown to police, they had collected samples of semen from both

"Are You Going to Dust for Prints?"

Because of TV series such as *CSI: Crime Scene Investigation*, which shows the details of forensic police work, the public has become much more savvy, says a Minneapolis police officer. But sometimes, he adds, there is a big difference between what is real and what is simply good television.

"I'll say right up front that I'm not complaining," he says. "But people have a different idea about what is realistic in our job. I have had calls from people who have had their garages broken into, or someone steals a bike or something off the front porch, and they say, 'Are you going to dust for prints?' It's hard to explain that the city barely has the budget to do the tests they need to do for crimes against persons, like rapes and murders, you know? Or you just want to tell them, it's probably kids in the neighborhood, and you're never going to get a match even if you run a print.

"My brother is a cop, too, and he took a call from an elderly couple who left their garage door open and when they came back, the lawn mower was gone. And you know what they asked him? If he thought there was any good DNA on the garage door. Boy, I wish it was that easy, you know? It's great having an informed public, but they ought to have a disclaimer on some of these shows, that it's not something we carry around in our back pocket."

Television shows like Crime Scene Investigation *have helped popularize forensic science.*

crime scenes. It was known then that about 85 percent of men are secretors, which means that they secrete proteins from their blood type in their other bodily fluids, including semen. At the time, police had hoped that the rapist or rapists were nonsecretors, which would place them in a much smaller group of suspects. Unfortunately for the police, however, the semen recovered from both scenes was that of a secretor.

Jeffreys tested the semen and verified what the police suspected—that they were dealing with one man, not two. He also tested a blood sample of the man whom police had in custody, a kitchen worker at a nearby mental hospital named Richard Buckland. The results shocked the police, for they showed clearly that Buckland was not the man who raped and murdered those girls.

To find the real killer, police asked every man who worked or lived in the village for a blood sample. They received forty-five hundred samples, and while Jeffreys began the laborious job of creating autorads of the samples, a rumor began to circulate in Narborough. A young man named Ian Kelly was overheard telling friends that he had done a favor for a coworker named Colin Pitchfork. Pitchfork, he said, was terrified of needles and had asked Kelly if he would give a blood test in his place.

When police heard this, they confronted Pitchfork and demanded a blood sample. The DNA matched that of the semen sample, and he confessed. Jeffreys was jubilant. Not only had his DNA fingerprint system worked by finding a dangerous killer, it had exonerated an innocent man.

Growing DNA

One of the drawbacks in early DNA analysis was that a fairly large sample was needed. If the bloodstain was too small, or if the cells within it had been damaged, the DNA could not be tested. Over the years, however, DNA testing has become much more sensitive. With a system called polymerase chain reaction (PCR), it is now possible to grow a complete DNA chain in the lab from a partial sample. After identifying the pattern from a small sample, PCR mimics a cell's ability to replicate its own DNA material.

PCR has totally revolutionized DNA use for forensic examiners. It is now possible to get DNA from even a single cell. "Information that previously was not of any value is of tremendous value now," says one medical examiner. "What we're looking for, like single hairs, small drops of blood, cigarette butts, traces of saliva from a telephone receiver—any of that material may contain DNA."[69]

Other forensic experts agree, saying that they continue to be surprised by the DNA information that can be gleaned from a few cells that never before would have been considered. Fingernail clippings and used paper tissues are processed for DNA. So are toothpicks, straws, and anything else that might have been in contact with a suspect's mouth, including a cell phone. Barry Fischer, director of the Los Angeles Sheriff Department's forensics lab, is one expert who admits being amazed by how far the limits of DNA have been pushed, saying, "You can get good DNA from a hatband or the nosepiece of a pair of glasses."[70]

DNA "Fingerprints" on File

Once DNA is collected from a crime scene, it is treated with chemicals to isolate it from the semen, blood, or other material so that it can be recorded as an autorad. The DNA information—that .1 percent of the DNA molecule that makes each person unique—is entered into a computer. Thus, it can later be compared with the DNA of anyone who becomes a suspect in the crime.

Each of the fifty states has its own DNA data bank, but there are different criteria regarding who is required to provide a sample. Every state requires convicted sex offenders to do so. Some states, however, bank DNA only from felons, while other states require a DNA sample from anyone arrested for any crime.

There is also a federal data bank, which was established by the FBI in 1994. The DNA equivalent of AFIS, the data bank is called the Combined DNA Index System, or CODIS. CODIS has DNA "fingerprints" of convicted criminals, as well as samples from unsolved crimes. As of March 2005, more than 2.3 million DNA fingerprints were on file.

Source: Federal Bureau of Investigation (www.fbi.gov).

CODIS Helps Solve Crimes

The FBI laboratory's Combined DNA Index System (CODIS) is a federal data bank that lets federal, state, and local crime labs exchange and compare the DNA profiles of convicted criminals, as well as DNA samples from unsolved crimes.

Since its inception in 1994, CODIS has assisted in thousands of investigations across the country. This map shows the number of investigations aided by CODIS through May 2005.

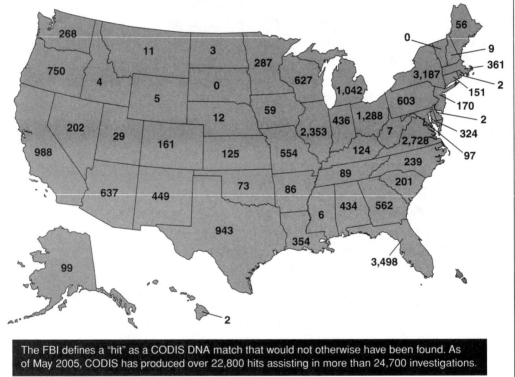

The FBI defines a "hit" as a CODIS DNA match that would not otherwise have been found. As of May 2005, CODIS has produced over 22,800 hits assisting in more than 24,700 investigations.

Cold Cases Solved

Between the improvements in DNA testing such as PCR and the rapidly growing data banks across the country, DNA fingerprinting has become an even more powerful forensic tool. This has become obvious not only in current investigations but in cold cases, or older, unsolved ones.

"You see older cases getting a second look now," says one Illinois attorney. "These cases could be from the early days of DNA testing, in the mid- to late

1980s, or they could even be cases from before DNA was even understood [as a forensic tool]. If the evidence is still around, and the guys in the lab can recover DNA from it—even just a little bit—it can be processed."[71]

The coldest of these cases was the 1968 rape and murder of thirteen-year-old Jane Durrua in New Jersey. She had been walking to her older sister's house when she decided to take a shortcut along nearby railroad tracks. Her bludgeoned body was found the next day near some tracks. The use of DNA as a forensic tool was unknown at the time, and even though examiners had recovered a semen stain, there was little they could do with it.

In 1999 the victim's two sisters begged detectives to reopen the case using new technology. The evidence was processed, and the DNA was recovered. While searching CODIS, examiners got a hit—a man currently serving time in prison for a sexual assault on a fifteen-year-old girl. Knowing that the murderer has been identified is gratifying to the victim's family, even though it took almost thirty-two years. "We feel wonderful," said her sister. "I never thought it would be solved."[72]

Freeing Innocent Prisoners

In addition to solving old cases, DNA evidence is also proving that some people currently serving time in prison are innocent of the crimes for which they were convicted. Most of these individuals served many years of a life sentence for murder or rape. Some, like Ronald Jones, were on death row. He was awaiting execution for a rape and murder that DNA analysis later proved he did not commit.

The victim was a woman found in an abandoned building on Chicago's South Side in 1985. Jones, who at the time was homeless and an alcoholic, was arrested and charged after police produced a signed confession from him. Semen recovered from the scene had been tested for DNA, but the results in 1985 were inconclusive. Even so, Jones was convicted and given the death penalty, despite the fact that he claimed that police physically coerced him to sign the confession.

After serving eight years on death row, Jones was exonerated when the evidence was examined again with current DNA technology. The test showed that the semen definitely was not Jones's, and in a retrial, he was given a pardon. The twelfth Illinois inmate in twelve years to be exonerated by DNA evidence, Jones was unquestionably relieved. "I just want people out there to know that some of these people [on death row] who say they are innocent, are innocent," he said in an interview in 2002. "Had it not been for DNA, who knows about me?"[73]

Baby 81

Not all forensics cases deal with crime. Some are concerned with legal disputes. Proof of a child's paternity is a frequent goal of DNA testing. In fact, in 2003 American laboratories alone performed almost 350,000 paternity DNA tests.

Soon after the devastating tsunami and earthquake occurred in South Asia in December 2004, there was a highly publicized case involving a question of not only the true father but the true mother of a baby in Sri Lanka. During the tsunami, tens of thousands of families were wrenched apart—children torn from parents' arms and swept away by the powerful waves. Many children perished, especially infants and toddlers. However, one baby in Sri Lanka who survived was discovered hours after the storm caked with mud and debris. He was brought to a makeshift hospital, and because he was the eighty-first patient admitted, he was known as Baby 81.

His parents, Jenita and Murugupillai, tried to claim him at the hospital, but his birth records had been destroyed, along with everything else in their

The Innocence Project

After DNA testing became more sophisticated, many prisoners requested new hearings using DNA tests, hoping that they could be exonerated by the evidence. In this excerpt from "It Wasn't Me," an article in the *London Independent*, Peter Neufeld and Barry Scheck give an example of one death row prisoner who was saved by DNA tests.

In 1982 a mother in Culpeper, Virginia, was raped and stabbed. Before she died, she told police that a black man was responsible. A year later, [Earl] Washington was arrested after assaulting his neighbor. During police questioning, he confessed to several crimes, including the Culpeper murder. His confession was deemed reliable, even though he didn't know the victim's race, age, or where she lived. Despite psychological analyses reporting Washington had an IQ of 69 . . . he was convicted and sentenced to death.

In August 1985, a month before his execution date, volunteer lawyers won a stay of execution. Six years later, the governor reluctantly allowed more sophisticated DNA tests which not only excluded Washington but implicated another man imprisoned for a similar crime. Washington was pardoned.

In 2001 Earl Washington was released from death row after DNA evidence exonerated him of a rape charge.

This Sri Lankan boy was reunited with his parents in the aftermath of the 2004 tsunami after DNA tests positively identified his parents.

home. To make matters more confusing, eight other couples claimed that baby as their own, arguing bitterly with one another in the hospital corridors.

A judge in Sri Lanka ordered that the child had to remain in the hospital until DNA tests could establish the baby's parentage. On February 16, 2005, more than seven weeks after the tsunami, the baby was reunited with his parents, Jenita and Murugupillai.

"They Scoured the Earth, These People"

It was terrorism, rather than a natural disaster, that resulted in the largest DNA project in U.S. history. The attacks on the World Trade Center in New York City on September 11, 2001, left thousands of families seeking official word that their loved ones had perished. It was extremely difficult for officials to provide that information. Because of the intense heat from the blaze and explosion, few of the victims could be identified by dental records, tattoos, or fingerprints.

Medical examiners from New York worked out of twelve refrigerated trailers set up next to Ground Zero. Bodies, or parts of bodies, that were unearthed in the debris were brought to the trailers until they could be processed for DNA. Every tiny bit of flesh or bone was refrigerated and tested against DNA that was taken from samples brought in by family members, such as hair or saliva from a victim's toothbrush.

The medical examiners and their technicians spared no effort in their quest to find usable DNA. Even people who have not yet had family members officially identified insist that the forensic teams are the unsung heroes at Ground Zero. "If there's one New York City agency that should be commended," says one man awaiting confirmation of his son's death, "it's them. They scoured the earth, these people."[74]

"Where There's DNA, There's Hope"
Although DNA once again demonstrated its value as a forensic tool at Ground Zero, in April 2005 it showed that it has limitations. After three and a half years, forensic examiners admitted that they could do no more. Of the nearly 20,000 body parts (sometimes dozens of parts per victim) that were found, experts still had identified only 1,593 people, or 58 percent of the victims.

Thousands of unidentified remains are still in storage, but most are in such poor condition that current DNA technology is not effective, say experts. "There came a time when the realization dawned on us that the degree of degradation was so great that we couldn't go further," admits one expert. "We did everything that was technologically feasible."[75]

A forensic scientist prepares a DNA sample for study. Advances in DNA technology will continue to make this forensic tool indispensable to crime investigation.

DNA technology has improved over the years, and perhaps in the future it will be sophisticated enough to identify the rest of the remains so that families can have that information about the fate of their loved ones. The remains yet unidentified have been dried and sealed in airtight bags for analysis, should that time ever come. Forensic expert Mark Stolorow says that is not a question of *if* but, rather, of *when.* "Far be it from a scientist to say that something is not scientifically possible," he says. "I am an optimist. Where there's DNA, there's hope."[76]

"Things Happen Quickly"

The growth of forensic technology over the past twenty years has been explosive, and there is no end in sight. "One thing I am excited about," says one technician, "is the trend toward more portable DNA units. In the past, as everyone knows, it's taken a great deal of time to get results back—weeks or months. That can slow down an investigation, and it can cost thousands of dollars for a single test. But in the future, I think there will be handheld DNA units that can give you a reading right on the spot. See a drop of blood, run it through the unit, and get your match in a few seconds. That's the future."[77]

"Things happen quickly," agrees one fingerprint technician, "and it's not just DNA. It's new software, new linkups between law enforcement agencies around the country, around the world. I think we're going to realize how much more computers can do for us, and how much faster things will go. One thing I know is that scientists of all kind are going to play a key role. The future is definitely not going to be a good time for the bad guys!"[78]

Notes

Introduction: Where Science Meets Crime

1. Dave, interview with the author, Minneapolis, MN, March 4, 2005.
2. David Fisher, *Hard Evidence: How Detectives Inside the FBI's Sci-Crime Lab Have Helped Solve America's Toughest Cases.* New York: Simon & Schuster, 1995, p. 11.

Chapter 1: Forensics and Fingerprints

3. Fisher, *Hard Evidence*, p. 128.
4. D.P. Lyle, *Forensics for Dummies.* Hoboken, NJ: Wiley, 2004, p. 74.
5. Richard, interview with the author, St. Paul, MN, March 18, 2005.
6. Richard, interview.
7. Dave, interview, March 4, 2005.
8. Quoted in N.E. Genge, *The Forensic Casebook.* New York: Ballantine, 2002, p. 31.
9. Quoted in Fisher, *Hard Evidence*, p. 131.
10. Quoted in Genge, *The Forensic Casebook*, pp. 34–35.
11. David Peterson, interview with the author, St. Paul, MN, April 20, 2005.
12. Peterson, interview.
13. Peterson, interview.
14. Derrick, interview with the author, Minneapolis, MN, March 19, 2005.
15. Dave, interview with the author, St. Paul, MN, November 4, 2004.
16. Peterson, interview.
17. Quoted in Fisher, *Hard Evidence*, p. 128.

Chapter 2: Who Are You?

18. Dave, interview, March 4, 2005.

19. Quoted in Genge, *The Forensic Casebook*, p. 158.
20. Michael McGee, interview with the author, St. Paul, MN, December 8, 2004.
21. Dave, interview, March 4, 2005.
22. Dale, interview with the author, St. Paul, MN, December 1, 2004.
23. Douglas Ubelaker and Henry Scammell, *Bones: A Forensic Detective's Casebook*. New York: Edward Burlingame, 1992, p. 27.
24. Greta, interview with the author, Minneapolis, MN, February 27, 2004.
25. Quoted in Genge, *The Forensic Casebook*, p. 282.
26. William R. Maples, *Dead Men Do Tell Tales*. New York: Doubleday, 1994, p. 108.
27. McGee, interview.
28. Maples, *Dead Men Do Tell Tales*, pp. 142–43.
29. Brian Innes, *Bodies of Evidence: The Fascinating World of Forensic Science and How It Helped Solve More than 100 True Crimes*. Pleasantville, NY: Reader's Digest, 2000, p. 90.
30. Quoted in Innes, *Bodies of Evidence*, p. 90.
31. Quoted in "The Talking Skull," *Forensic Files*, Court TV, aired May 3, 2005.

Chapter 3: Crime Solving Through Chemistry

32. Dave, interview, March 4, 2005.
33. Lyle, *Forensics for Dummies*, p. 254.
34. Dave Tebow, telephone interview, December 2, 2004.
35. Fisher, *Hard Evidence*, p. 30.
36. Quoted in Cathy Newman, "12 Toxic Tales," *National Geographic*, May 2005, p. 20.
37. Quoted in Innes, *Bodies of Evidence*, p. 164.
38. Quoted in Newman, "12 Toxic Tales," p. 10.
39. Quoted in Newman, "12 Toxic Tales," p. 19.
40. Tebow, interview.
41. Tebow, interview.
42. Quoted in Cyril Wecht, ed., *Crime Scene Investigation*. Pleasantville, NY: Reader's Digest, 2004, p. 71.
43. Quoted in Fisher, *Hard Evidence*, p. 36.
44. Quoted in Fisher, *Hard Evidence*, p. 36.
45. Quoted in Elizabeth Rosenthal, "American Doctors Helped

Identify Ukraine Leader's Poisoning," *New York Times*, March 13, 2005, p. I13.

Chapter 4: Questioned Documents

46. Leland, interview with the author, Minneapolis, MN, May 1, 2005.
47. Quoted in Kenneth Terrell, "Mystery Map Stumps Scholars—Again," *U.S. News & World Report*, August 12, 2002, p. 52.
48. Quoted in SkyGaze, "Hitler's Diaries," April 2004. www.skygaze.com/content/mysteries/Hitler.shtml.
49. Quoted in Fisher, *Hard Evidence*, p. 212.
50. Quoted in Genge, *The Forensic Casebook*, p. 120.
51. Celia, telephone interview, May 2, 2005.
52. Quoted in Fisher, *Hard Evidence*, p. 205.
53. Don Foster, *Author Unknown: On the Trail of Anonymous*. New York: Henry Holt, 2000, p. 99.

Chapter 5: Crime Scene Impressions

54. Steve Banning, interview with the author, St. Paul, MN, November 9, 2004.
55. Dave, interview, March 4, 2005.
56. Quoted in Fisher, *Hard Evidence*, p. 222.
57. Innes, *Bodies of Evidence*, p. 135.
58. Dencell, telephone interview, April 22, 2005.
59. Lyle, *Forensics for Dummies*, p. 101.
60. John Houde, *Crime Lab: A Guide for Nonscientists*. Ventura, CA: Calico, 1999, p. 158.
61. Banning, interview.
62. Tebow, interview.
63. Dave, interview, March 4, 2005.
64. Dencell, interview.
65. Dencell, interview.
66. Dave, interview, March 4, 2005.
67. Tebow, interview.

Chapter 6: The DNA Fingerprint

68. Quoted in Richard Willing, "White House Seeks to Expand DNA Database," *USA Today*, April 15, 2004. www.usatoday.com/news/washington/2004-04-15-dna-usat_x.htm.

69. McGee, interview.
70. Quoted in Amy Lennard Goehner, Lina Lofaro, and Kate Novack, "Where *CSI* Meets Real *Law and Order*," *Time*, November 8, 2004, p. 69.
71. Pete Young, telephone interview, April 22, 2005.
72. Quoted in Robert Hanley, "DNA Leads to Arrest in '68 Rape and Murder of Girl, 13," *New York Times*, June 17, 2004, p. B5.
73. Quoted in Fran Spielman, "Former Death Row Inmate to Get $2.2 Million," *Chicago Sun-Times*, December 16, 2003, p. 22.
74. Quoted in Stevenson Swanson, "DNA Project to Identify Sept. 11 Victims Pauses," *Chicago Tribune*, April 24, 2005. www.dailynews.yahoo.com/s/chitribts/20050424/ts_chicago trib/dnaprojecttoidentifysept11victimspauses.
75. Quoted in Swanson, "DNA Project."
76. Quoted in Swanson, "DNA Project."
77. Dencell, interview.
78. Richard, interview.

For Further Reading

Books

Andrea Campbell, *Forensic Science: Evidence, Clues, and Investigation*. Philadelphia: Chelsea House, 2000. Helpful bibliography and index.

Colin Evans, *Murder 2: The Second Casebook of Forensic Detection*. Hoboken, NJ: Wiley, 2004. Very readable account of some famous crimes and the ways forensic science helped solve them. Good timeline showing landmarks of forensics.

Tina Kafka, *DNA on Trial*. San Diego: Lucent, 2005. Very good information on the effects of DNA technology, as well as the growth of DNA fingerprinting, on law enforcement. Excellent bibliography.

David Owen, *Hidden Evidence: Forty True Crimes and How Forensic Science Helped Solve Them*. Willowdale, ON, Canada: Firefly, 2002. Excellent photographs and a helpful glossary of forensic terms.

Richard Platt, *Crime Scene: The Ultimate Guide to Forensic Science*. London: DK, 2003. Includes color photographs showing various aspects of forensic science and a helpful timeline of breakthroughs in forensics.

Periodicals

Bergen County, NJ Record, "No Joy for Baby 81's Parents," March 3, 2005.

Gerald McKelvey, "Ex Prof: I Mailed Poison," *Newsday*, June 10, 1987.

Amanda Ripley, "The DNA Dragnet," *Time*, January 24, 2005.

Betsy Streisand, "100 Percent False," *U.S. News & World Report*, August 26, 2002.

Works Consulted

Books

David Fisher, *Hard Evidence: How Detectives Inside the FBI's Sci-Crime Lab Have Helped Solve America's Toughest Cases.* New York: Simon & Schuster, 1995. Excellent information on toxicology and DNA screening.

Don Foster, *Author Unknown: On the Trail of Anonymous.* New York: Henry Holt, 2000. Fascinating first-person account of a linguistic analyst and his examination of documents such as the "Unabomber Manifesto."

N.E. Genge, *The Forensic Casebook.* New York: Ballantine, 2002. Very readable, with great sections on fingerprint analysis and DNA fingerprinting.

John Houde, *Crime Lab: A Guide for Nonscientists.* Ventura, CA: Calico, 1999. Excellent photography, with a helpful section on DNA fingerprints.

Brian Innes, *Bodies of Evidence: The Fascinating World of Forensic Science and How It Helped Solve More than 100 True Crimes.* Pleasantville, NY: Reader's Digest, 2000. Excellent sections on fingerprinting and DNA evidence.

D.P. Lyle, *Forensics for Dummies.* Hoboken, NJ: Wiley, 2004. Very readable, with interesting chapters on tool and impression analysis as well as on DNA typing.

William R. Maples, *Dead Men Do Tell Tales.* New York: Doubleday, 1994. Very readable, with helpful photographs.

Douglas Ubelaker and Henry Scammell, *Bones: A Forensic Detective's Casebook.* New York: Edward Burlingame, 1992. Anecdotal, with good information about using bones and teeth for identification.

Cyril Wecht, ed., *Crime Scene Investigation.* Pleasantville, NY: Reader's Digest, 2004. Excellent section on fingerprinting, with very readable text.

Periodicals and Broadcast Media

Amy Lennard Goehner, Lina Lofaro, and Kate Novack, "Where *CSI* Meets Real *Law and Order*," *Time*, November 8, 2004.

Robert Hanley, "DNA Leads to Arrest in '68 Rape and Murder of Girl, 13," *New York Times*, June 17, 2004.

National Geographic, "In the Morgue with Al and Marcella," May 2005.

Peter Neufeld and Barry Scheck, "It Wasn't Me," *London Independent*, June 1, 2003.

Cathy Newman, "12 Toxic Tales," *National Geographic*, May 2005.

Elizabeth Rosenthal, "American Doctors Helped Identify Ukraine Leader's Poisoning," *New York Times*, March 13, 2005.

Fran Spielman, "Former Death Row Inmate to Get $2.2 Million," *Chicago Sun-Times*, December 16, 2003.

"The Talking Skull," *Forensic Files,* Court TV, aired May 3, 2005.

Kenneth Terrell, "Mystery Map Stumps Scholars—Again," *U.S. News & World Report*, August 12, 2002.

Internet Sources

SkyGaze, "Hitler's Diaries," April 2004. www.skygaze.com/content/mysteries/Hitler.shtml.

Stevenson Swanson, "DNA Project to Identify Sept. 11 Victims Pauses," *Chicago Tribune*, April 24, 2005. www.dailynews.yahoo.com/s/chitribts/20050424/ts_chicagotrib/dnaproject toidentifysept11victimspauses.

Richard Willing, "White House Seeks to Expand DNA Database," *USA Today*, April 15, 2004. www.usatoday.com/news/washington/2004-04-15-dna-usat_x.htm.

Web Sites

Federal Bureau of Investigation (www.fbi.gov/hq/lab/lab home.htm). This site has activities and information for students in grades 6 through 12, including participating in a crime case from beginning to end.

Innocence Project (www.innocenceproject.org). Based at the Benjamin N. Cardozo School of Law in New York, this group works to help current inmates get new trials based on new DNA technology.

Zeno's Forensic Science Site (http://forensic.to/forensic. html). This site contains an extensive listing of links to all aspects of forensic science—from document analysis and DNA to ballistics and forensic psychology.

Index

Picture Credits

About the Author

Gail B. Stewart received her undergraduate degree from Gustavus Adolphus College in St. Peter, Minnesota. She did her graduate work in English, linguistics, and curriculum study at the College of St. Thomas and the University of Minnesota. She taught English and reading for more than ten years.

She has written over ninety books for young people, including a series for Lucent Books called The Other America. She has written many books on historical topics such as World War I and the Warsaw ghetto.

Stewart and her husband live in Minneapolis with their three sons, Ted, Elliot, and Flynn; two dogs; and a cat. When Stewart is not writing, she enjoys reading, walking, and watching her sons play soccer.